Use the power of feedback to write a better book

Belinda Pollard

SMALL BLUE DOG
PUBLISHING

Copyright © Belinda Pollard 2019

usefulwritingtips.com

Use the Power of Feedback to Write a Better Book was originally published as *Beta Reader Superhero*.

First published in Australia in 2019 by Small Blue Dog Publishing,
PO Box 310, Lawnton Queensland 4501, Australia
smallbluedog.com
ask@smallbluedog.com

ISBN
Paperback: 978-0-6482672-5-6
Epub: 978-0-9945002-6-7
Mobi: 978-0-6482672-6-3

All rights reserved. No part of this book may be reproduced or transmitted by any person or entity (including Google, Amazon or similar organizations), in any form or by any means, electronic or mechanical, including photocopying, recording, scanning or by any information storage and retrieval system, without prior permission in writing from the publisher.

 A catalogue record for this book is available from the National Library of Australia

Edition 1

Typeset in Adobe Garamond Pro and Myriad Pro

Cover images via Bigstock copyright © shawn_h, Robyn Mackenzie
Author images copyright © Tania Jovanovic

Copy editor & proofreader Alix Kwan

Beta Reader Superhero® is a registered trademark
of Belinda Pollard and Small Blue Dog Publishing Pty Ltd

*For all the patient, generous, insightful people
whose feedback makes me a better writer, book by book.*

Acknowledgments

THANK YOU TO MY BLOG READERS, workshop participants, survey respondents, editing and coaching clients and beta readers across many years and many projects. You have inspired and challenged me, and shaped the content of this book. You are the reason it exists.

Thank you to all my author friends who have helped me at various stages during the development of this book, and sharpened my thinking about how to make the content more useful.

Thank you to the team of beta readers who waded through my messy first draft and poured wisdom and encouragement over me and my manuscript, helping me see practicalities and possibilities.

- Debbie Young, author of the Sophie Sayers Village Mysteries.
- Jodie Lane, author of the Turning Points time travel adventure series.
- Molly Greene, author of the Gen Delacourt Mysteries.
- Sally Vince, developmental and copy editor.

Thank you to my editor and proofreader, Alix Kwan, for your insight, intelligent suggestions, kindness and good humor. You didn't just correct my typos and inaccuracies; you made it a better and more useful book.

Thank you to my darling mother, Barbara Pollard. If not for your detailed feedback, tireless practical support, emotional

Use the power of feedback to write a better book

encouragement, and—eventually—exuberant nagging this book would *still* not be finished.

And finally, thank you to the Divine Communicator who invented language and the creative spark within the human soul.

Contents

Acknowledgments　v

PART 1:
The power of feedback in writing and publishing　1

Chapter 1. Why writing feedback matters　2
- The meaning of the term "beta reader."
- The results of my survey about writing feedback.
- How my experiences shaped my feedback strategy, and how my discoveries might help you.
- Tips for getting what you need from this book, as fast as possible.
- The three pillars of my 3H Feedback strategy: Humility, Honesty and Heart.
- What I think about rules.

Chapter 2. The basics　12
- Definitions and descriptions—what a beta reader is and is not.
- Types of books beta readers can help with.
- Why beta readers don't replace professional editors.

Chapter 3. The ideal beta reader　26
- Demographics of the ideal beta reader.
- Personality traits and relevant experience.
- Reading and writing characteristics to look for.
- How much publishing knowledge should a beta reader have?

Chapter 4. Where to find the right beta readers for you 39

- How to network with other writers to find people who are a good match for your writing style and might enjoy helping you.
- How to find specialists in a particular topic.
- Where to look for beta readers who are *not* writers.
- When to start looking.

PART 2:
Managing the feedback process for your book 55

Chapter 5. When to use beta readers 56

- Where beta readers can add value in each phase of creating a book, complementing tasks a professional editor might do.
- When to use or avoid beta readers, depending on your goals and level of experience.
- Whether to engage your beta team all at once, or spread them out over the project timeline.

Chapter 6. Issuing the initial invitation 77

- Attitudes that create an effective beta reading process, and ones that work against us.
- Tips for making the initial request.
- How many to ask.
- Content warnings.

Chapter 7. Building a beta feedback relationship 85

- Setting the tone.
- Fine-tuning the schedule.
- Formats to offer, and formats to ask for.
- Asking for testimonials.

Chapter 8. Creating a productive briefing document   96

- Choosing the discussion issues that will be most valuable for your manuscript—big picture versus fine detail.
- Wording your questions in a way that helps your beta readers.
- Organizing questions to help simplify your revision process.

PART 3:
What to do with the feedback you receive   113

Chapter 9. How to apply the feedback you receive   114

- Different instinctive reactions to beta feedback, and attitudes that can help.
- The importance of time and space.
- Several techniques for weighing the results.

Where to now?   132

Glossary   134

Index   136

About the Author   139

Fun and useful gifts for beta readers and writers   140

Also by Belinda Pollard   141

PART 1:
The power of feedback in writing and publishing

....

The value of writing feedback, some basic definitions, traits of an ideal "beta reader," and where to find the right people to give you the feedback you need.

Chapter 1. Why writing feedback matters

When I was wrestling with my debut murder mystery, *Poison Bay*, I had been writing in a vacuum, and needed an outside perspective on whether the manuscript was working. I was hesitant to seek feedback at first, but became more committed to the process as I saw the power of it.

I now seek feedback for all my own publishing projects, and recommend it to my editing clients. It's become about much more than just problem-solving a particular manuscript. Wrestling with feedback has changed not just my books, but *me*. The process has made me a better writer, and a better editor. If you are willing to open your mind and experiment, I believe effective feedback can make a powerful difference to your writing career, too.

In this chapter...

- The meaning of the term "beta reader."
- The results of my survey about writing feedback.
- How my experiences shaped my feedback strategy, and how my discoveries might help you.
- Tips for getting what you need from this book, as fast as possible.
- The three pillars of my 3H Feedback strategy: Humility, Honesty and Heart.

- What I think about rules.

The term "beta reader"

Many authors have pre-publication "first readers" for their manuscripts, and they call them various things. For convenience, in this book we'll use the term "beta reader." I'd never heard this term till about ten years ago, but the concept is not new. Even Jane Austen apparently read her manuscripts aloud to her sister.

A beta reader is simply someone who gives a writer useful feedback on their manuscript.

The beta version of anything is the test version. The term seems to have been borrowed from the software industry, where "beta testers" help iron out bugs before new software is released.

When I refer to a "beta reader" in this book, I mean:

- **an amateur, rather than a trained professional**
- **a volunteer, rather than someone who is paid.**

Others may use the term differently, which is fine. I don't own the words! However, keeping these distinctions in mind will help you get the most out of this particular book.

Beta is the second letter of the Greek alphabet (alpha-beta), pronounced bee-ta, bay-ta or bet-ta in different parts of the world. I'm in Australia and I say bee-ta. (A friend who says bay-ta told me that when she hears me say "bee-ta reader" she thinks of people with sticks beating that manuscript into shape, which made me laugh, but is not a process endorsed by this book.)

My survey

While I was writing this book, I conducted a survey about beta reading through my website smallbluedog.com. I received a rush of responses—50 in the first two hours alone. Feedback is clearly an issue that matters to people and with which they've struggled at times. Clear themes emerged:*

- 31% had trouble finding the right beta readers—skilled, familiar with their genre, and who understood what was expected of them.
- 30% said feedback often arrived too late to be useful, or not at all.
- 16% said their beta readers were too nice and avoided giving honest feedback for fear of hurting the writer's feelings.
- 8% couldn't get enough detail from feedback.
- 5% were frustrated that beta readers insisted on correcting typos when they'd been asked to look at big-picture issues.

Clearly, all is not rosy in the feedback garden. The purpose of this book is to address these problems and find effective solutions.

---

* My survey used what statisticians would call a self-selected sample, so I make no claims that the results are unbiased or can be said, statistically, to represent all writers everywhere. However, the survey did reveal the experiences and thoughts of a sizable group of people who have a strong interest in writing feedback. The results mentioned here were responses to the open-ended first question: "What is the biggest problem you face with beta readers?" The answers to this question represent the issues that were top of mind for 146 writers.

My story

My long and quirky journey through the publishing industry has shaped my approach to beta readers and manuscript feedback. Back in the 80s, I put on my leg warmers and went to university to study Communication, which included editing for mass media and the psychology of language. I became a radio and television journalist. Having my work critiqued as part of the news collection process was expected and normal.

I want to encourage you to see critique as natural, too. Seeking feedback doesn't mark you as a novice; it says you're professional.

In the mid-90s, I followed a personal passion into Theology studies. It was meant to be one year, but four years later I had an honors degree, and a job as book editor with a specialist publisher in Sydney, Australia. My boss mentored me, trusted me and empowered me. She let me make my own mistakes and discover my own strengths.

She's part of the reason I want to empower you to learn to trust yourself and find your unique strengths as both a writer and a beta reader for other writers.

At that publishing house I first encountered beta readers—although we didn't call them that. Each manuscript went out to specialists, or sometimes to a general reader. We evaluated their feedback and discussed it with the author.

That's why I want to encourage you to think of your beta readers' feedback as something you weigh carefully and think about creatively, not something you just obey.

I grew into an editor of content and structure, not just a typo corrector—seeing potential miscommunication and suggesting solutions. I discovered I could give useful feedback to people who knew more about their field than I did.

I hope you can be open to receiving useful ideas from beta readers less knowledgeable or experienced than yourself. When you provide feedback for other writers, even if you feel intimidated you can provide useful insights to experienced writers.

Fast forward a couple of decades. I've been in publishing for twenty years, and have worked on some exceptional books by authors in various fields. I've also become an author myself, with multiple books in various genres that have been traditionally published or indie published. I never stop learning. As an editor and writing coach, each time I recommend beta feedback for my clients I experiment, observe and customize the process. As an author, my beta readers continue to open my eyes to new possibilities. As a beta reader exchanging unpaid feedback with other authors, I wrestle with new ways to make my feedback more useful.

Whether you are a new writer or are experienced and successful, please let me encourage you not to get locked into one "right" way. Great results come when we experiment, observe, and continually refine the feedback process as both writer and beta reader.

Tips for getting the most out of this book in the shortest possible time

You're busy, so I've deliberately constructed this book for easy access. Dive deep if you prefer, or dip in and out to grab useful ideas as you need them. These are some features I hope will make it more useful:

- I've included a comprehensive Table of Contents at the start and an alphabetical Index at the end, to help you find the answer to the question you have right now, or to locate cross references to extra information.

- Each chapter ends with a quick recap—for skimming or later reminders.
- To make this book more useful for those who are just starting to use beta readers, or have found their past efforts frustrating and ineffective, I will explain the recommended steps simply but fully.
- Occasionally, information is included in several places where it's useful and applicable, to save you hunting.
- Don't expect to see "whom" very often. I've written in conversational English to make the book a fast and easy read.
- If you're not sure of the meaning of a word, consult the glossary on p. 134. Note that some of these words can be used different ways. The glossary will show you how I've used that word in this book.
- My strategy for beta readers is unique to me. If something in a later section puzzles you, please refer back to Part 1, which lays the foundation.

Let me tell you a story...

 I get useful ideas when I "reverse engineer" case studies about other people's experiences, by unpacking what they did and looking for principles or techniques that I could adapt to my situation. That's why I will tell a lot of my own and other people's stories in this book. Some are brief; some are detailed case studies. Look for them where you see this speech bubble icon.

Many of the stories emerged from the survey of writers I conducted in early 2017. Authors who are mentioned by only a first name are survey respondents who gave permission for their comments to be used in this book anonymously. Their names have been changed for privacy purposes.

Other comments from personal interviews are also used by permission.

POWER TIPS

 Look for the rocket icon to find industry secrets, surprising insights and the occasional wild idea.

3H Feedback:
Humility + Honesty + Heart

There are three pillars to my strategy for feedback: Humility, Honesty and Heart. I call this 3H Feedback.

3H•Humility

As **authors**, humility helps us to accept that we need help, reach out to ask for it in a way that beta readers find attractive, and listen carefully to the feedback when it comes—even if it's hard to hear.

When we become **beta readers** for other authors, humility reminds us that we don't know everything about this book, this author, the publishing industry, or readers worldwide, and helps us give feedback without any taint of superiority that could intimidate or alienate the person receiving it.

3H•Honesty

As **authors**, honesty helps us see our writing more clearly, and speak to our beta readers with a transparency that actually helps them get past any inadequacy they may feel about being a beta reader. It helps remove inhibitions that can cramp the feedback process.

When we become **beta readers** for other authors, honesty helps us to avoid empty flattery but also to look diligently for the good in a manuscript. The resulting feedback is more likely to genuinely empower the writer.

3H•Heart

As **authors**, heart gives us the courage to confront the flaws in our manuscript, the purity of purpose to know which suggestions to adopt and which to reject or adapt, and the tenacity to wade in and do those rewrites.

When we become **beta readers** for other authors, heart helps us handle writers' dreams with kindness and gentleness, avoid sarcasm, and make our feedback so much easier to hear and act upon.

What are your goals?

If you are seeking a **traditional publisher**, an effective beta feedback process can help you bring out your unique voice more strongly, get your manuscript off the slush pile, and capture the attention of an agent.

If you plan to **self-publish**, beta readers can help you produce an industry-standard book. I still believe editors are necessary, and always hire one on my own indie projects. However, I find that beta readers can complement the editing process and expand its scope, and will include some tips about these possibilities.

The number of beta readers you have, how you recruit them, what you ask them to do, and how you use their feedback might change over your writing career and vary from project to project.

Rule 1: There are no rules

I share my observations, experiences, tips and suggestions in this book, but I don't make rules. I don't believe there is a right and wrong way to do it. We each must develop our own strategies and techniques.

How I ended up writing a book about feedback

This book grew out of a blog post I wrote at smallbluedog.com which got much more attention than I was expecting, and generated a series of blog posts. Journal articles, workshops and webinars followed. It became clear to me that a lot of writers struggled to get effective feedback, and yet it was something they really wanted. I was surprised by how many were frustrated by bad results when I'd found the beta feedback process strengthening for my own writing. I accidentally became a passionate advocate for beta readers and harnessing the power of effective feedback.

My approach was not learned in any school. I'm a developmental/structural editor and author who has experimented with my own beta feedback process over many years, continually evaluating, rethinking and refining my methods and my expectations.

This book goes far beyond the content of those original blog posts, not only because it covers a wider scope, but also because I've learned so much more through continuous development since that first article way back in 2012.

I've made plenty of mistakes on both sides of the feedback process—as both writer and beta reader—but may I say to you: don't fear the mistakes. On the other side of them lies the best literary-feedback adventures yet to come. Mistakes are not a sign of failure, but a possibility to investigate.

> **A fruitful, well-managed beta feedback process can be the difference between an ordinary book and an exceptional one—not because it changes the book, but because it changes the *writer*.**

I'm a much better writer today than I was five years ago, and my beta readers have had a lot to do with that. I will be an even better writer in five years' time, and again my beta readers will play a central part in that.

A quick recap

- When I refer to a beta reader, I mean an amateur who gives feedback for free. Others may use the term differently, which is fine.
- My background has helped me to see feedback as normal and valuable, and empowered me to develop new strengths as a writer. I want to encourage you to find similar value in it.
- The pillars of my 3H Feedback strategy—Humility, Honesty and Heart—help us as writers and when we are beta reading for someone else.
- There are no rules about beta feedback. We must each develop our own methods.
- An effective beta feedback process changes not just the manuscript but the *writer*.

Chapter 2. The basics

WHAT YOU READ HERE MAY DIFFER from the way some other people use beta readers. That's okay; there's room for all of us. As I've said previously, the approach I've developed has been heavily influenced by my work as a developmental and structural editor since the mid-90s. My goal is to draw from that experience to give you ideas and inspiration that will help you build a personal, customized feedback process for your writing.

Creative pursuits by their very nature require methods that are individual and organic. Your own unique strategy—tried, tested and tweaked over time—is the one that will help you continue to grow into the writer *you* were born to be.

In this chapter...

- Definitions and descriptions—what a beta reader is and is not.
- Types of books beta readers can help with.
- Why beta readers don't replace professional editors.

What is the role of a beta reader?

- A beta reader is **like a test pilot** for your manuscript. They take it for a spin, see how it handles for them, and give you a subjective response which you must then interpret.

- A beta reader is **like a mirror** in a department store change room—the type that fold to let you see yourself from the side and behind. Beta readers open your eyes to things you didn't know about your writing and your manuscript. They reflect back to you how your writing technique and your manuscript affects them as a reader.
- The beta feedback process is **like resistance training at a gym.** As you push back against the pressure created by the feedback, you grow your writing muscle and your commitment to what you really believe about your manuscript.
- When I talk about a beta reader in this book, I mean **someone who critiques for free**. When I'm talking about a paid professional I'll call them an editor, proofreader or writing coach. (Others may use the terms differently.)
- **Often, a beta reader is a fellow writer**. They tend to be more willing because they understand how much you value feedback, and their knowledge of the writing process can be handy.
- **Sometimes, a beta reader will not be a writer** but just someone who enjoys books, or a target reader for a particular book. With children's books, for example, you will want some children and other readers who understand children in the right age range—teachers, parents or babysitters. In some forms of non-fiction, you might choose an expert in that field, or a likely consumer of your type of information. And sometimes it's good to have a couple of beta readers who haven't read all the blog posts forbidding adverbs and prologues, who can respond to your manuscript with an open heart and mind. Some people also have success with beta readers who are

new to the genre—they see it quite differently and can be the catalyst for a brilliant idea.

- Ideally, **a beta reader has never seen the manuscript before** and is given the complete manuscript, rather than being drip-fed chapters. This helps them experience it in a similar way to a member of the public reading the book.
- **Some writers have arrangements with a beta buddy or critique partner** who gives earlier feedback on segments of a manuscript. This is also useful, but in a different way to someone who reads the whole book in context.

What a beta reader is NOT

- A beta reader is **not a guide, a leader, a fixer, or the captain of your manuscript**. You must always be in charge. Manage the feedback process so that they help you clarify your own vision and voice, rather than imposing their vision and voice on your book.
- **A beta reader is not an editor**. I don't recommend letting your beta reader change your manuscript—although some might make notes in it for convenience and clarity. If they do so, ask them to make sure they flag anything they've changed.
- A beta reader is **not a herding dog**, nipping at your heels and telling you which way you are allowed to go. A beta reader is more like a watch dog, alerting you to a danger in your manuscript that your senses hadn't detected, so you can choose how you'll deal with the situation. You might do nothing; maybe when you investigate further you'll realize it's not a problem you're concerned about.

- **Writers' groups that have group feedback sessions are not the same thing as beta readers**, although some people do find their beta readers at writers' groups. A beta reader ideally reads a manuscript by themselves, and responds as an individual, unswayed by the groupthink that can occur in a crowd.

What is an alpha reader?

Some people talk about alpha readers as those who read a very early manuscript. For others, alpha readers give feedback on the final version.

There are no rules about any of this terminology, only usage—and that is quite recent. Therefore, please feel free to use the terminology any way you wish, so long as it helps you and makes sense to the people you are talking to.

However, for the purposes of this book let's sidestep confusion. "Beta" refers to the *manuscript* rather than the reader. **In this book, any draft manuscript is a beta manuscript, and anyone who reads a manuscript for free any time before publication is a beta reader.** I don't personally use the term "alpha reader" or differentiate between different types of pre-publication volunteer readers.

Which types of books can I use beta readers for?

Most books benefit from beta reader feedback. Academic feedback is a specialty area that we won't explore in this book, although you may find some of the general principles useful.

We'll focus on books for a general readership, divided into three broad categories:

1. **Fiction**—stories that are "made up." A novel is a fictional story. Genres include fantasy, crime, romance, adventure, horror, children's, young adult, new adult, humor, sci-fi, dystopian, historical, western, paranormal, and many more.

2. **Memoir**—based on the author's memories. This means it is a type of fact (non-fiction). However, as creative non-fiction, a surprising number of the principles of fiction writing also apply. It's a story based on themes, rather than a blow-by-blow history of people or events. It's not always easy to draw a clear line between memoir and the other life-story genres (biography and autobiography). However, memoir tends to deliberately engage the imagination and emotions of both writer and reader more than biography or autobiography do. Memoir's focus goes beyond the facts and historical impact of a life.

3. **Non-fiction**—based on fact or information. Includes how-to, self-help, textbooks, recipe books, Bible commentaries, literary commentaries, history, formal biography/autobiography, reference books, and more.

Others may describe these labels differently (there are no rules!), but when you see them used in this book, the above definitions are what I mean.

Beta feedback serves a different purpose for each genre. Therefore, how you respond to feedback will also differ between genres.

- **Fiction and creative non-fiction such as memoir**: the purpose of the manuscript is to entertain and possibly inspire—goals that are highly subjective. The beta feedback process is about seeing your creative vision reflected back to you through other eyes, so that you can imagine ways to make it more powerful.

- **Non-fiction**: the purpose of the manuscript is to inform, enable, educate and/or inspire. Beta readers help you see what others will find useful. Clarity and usefulness are key. The outcomes tend to be more measurable; for example, if the book is *How to Build a Rabbit Hutch*, a reader can tell you whether or not they would be able to build a rabbit hutch after reading your book. Therefore, even though there will be times you still make a careful choice to disregard beta feedback, you might tend to look more diligently for solutions when a beta reader tells you the book didn't serve the stated purpose in their case.

I often give a non-fiction manuscript a robust haircut in response to beta feedback, but my reaction might be more subtle in the case of creative writing.

Beta readers versus professional editors

Beta readers don't replace professional editors, proofreaders and writing coaches. I see the roles as complementary.

In my own publishing projects, I use both beta readers and editors, but I use them to achieve different things. For my coaching and editing clients, I usually recommend a combination of beta feedback, professional editors and proofreaders.

Let's imagine improving a manuscript were like one of these two tasks: trying to improve personal appearance, or renovating your house.

- **Beta readers** might be like fellow members of a sporting team or exercise class. They encourage and motivate you, and they might even show you how to correct your technique with a certain movement. Compared to home renovation, beta readers might be like the friends who give you feedback on your color and design choices, and even pitch in to help you lift something heavy. Beta readers help you get more muscle or beauty in your manuscript to become a stronger writer overall, but it's still you that has to do the work. You are limited by the extent of your own ability, schedule constraints and level of commitment, as well as the ability of your beta reader to give useful feedback.

- A **writing coach** might be like a personal fitness trainer or a teacher of renovation techniques who has seen the state of your house. They help you target your specific weaknesses, goals and opportunities with customized techniques, and help you further develop your writing strengths.

- **Editors and proofreaders** might be like surgeons or professional makeup artists, or in the case of home renovation, like skilled tradesmen who make your plans a reality. They will do the work for you; the depth of their work depends on your requirements and budget. Someone who's had good cosmetic surgery looks fresher but is still recognizable, and a good professional renovation on your home still feels like home. In a similar way, your professionally-edited manuscript should still sound like you, only better.

Developmental editing

As I'll discuss further in Chapter 5, I see beta readers as particularly useful in the **developmental stages** of rewriting and self-editing a manuscript. This book is largely about helping you make the most of beta feedback during those phases.

Following are some generalizations about the potential differences between an experienced developmental editor and a beta reader:

- Beta readers might identify problems that you have no idea how to solve, but an editor will either give you suggested ways to solve it, or sometimes even do it for you if you are paying for a full developmental edit.
- The editor might be better able than the beta reader to diagnose the underlying causes of a particular problem, and be wiser and more subtle regarding potential solutions.
- The editor might notice more flaws, be less likely to miss important flaws, and be less inclined to fixate on minor issues.
- The editor might be better at generalizing to a larger readership rather than simply focusing on their own preferences.
- The editor might be less inclined to be swayed by spurious "rules" that do the rounds of the writing community, such as "no adverbs," "no prologues," and so on.

As I said, these are generalizations. You might be blessed with a beta reader who has highly-specialized skills. But even then, an editor will generally be able to spend more time on your manuscript, and therefore go deeper and wider with their analysis.

To make the most of beta feedback, given these limitations:

- engage multiple beta readers so you get a cross-section of opinions
- look carefully when a beta reader identifies a flaw, in case there might be other possible causes for their reaction

- give yourself plenty of time to weigh up your reactions to feedback
- do some research to figure out how to fix things that might initially perplex you.

Copy editing

As for **copy editing**—fixing of grammar, spelling, punctuation, flow—I've not often seen good results emerge when writers assign this task to beta readers. It's a rare beta reader who is good at all the tasks of copy editing, even if they think they are, or who is able to spend the many hours it takes to check every word in every sentence in every paragraph. And when a writer is not naturally good at grammar, it can be hard for them to tell whether or not the beta reader has done a good job.

You will develop your own procedure based on your experience, personality and priorities, but this is how I use both amateur and professional feedback in my own writing projects. Yes, I use a lot of feedback! Both traditional and self-publishing have a similar number of feedback layers for me—it's just that for self-publishing I'm paying for it, whereas in traditional publishing the publisher provides much of it.

For my **traditionally-published books**, my approach varies by genre.

My traditionally-published **non-fiction** has generally been commissioned. Because I'm writing to a detailed brief, I tend to use a light beta feedback process—perhaps just one or two opinions on the final draft, or a discussion on an earlier draft if I'm trying to solve a particular problem. I don't hire professionals to edit my commissioned non-fiction because the publisher's brief has shaped the content, my final drafts are fairly clean of basic errors, and the publisher will assign an editor and proofreader.

For **fiction**, when I took some steps down the traditional publishing route before opting to go indie, I engaged multiple beta readers as well as a professional at the big-picture level, to help me make my manuscript as competitive as possible. (A publisher would have assigned an editor or editors, and a proofreader.)

For my **indie* books**, I use a team approach:

- At least two or three (and up to seven or eight) beta readers, some of whom might be specialists in a particular field. Developmental editing is my superpower, but it's still hard to see all the possibilities in my own work. I find that beta feedback helps me see past my self-blindness in that regard.
- I hire a professional copy editor to edit my final draft before typesetting.
- Immediately before publication, I engage a proofreader to make the final check.

For my **indie fiction and creative non-fiction**, as opposed to non-fiction, I add a further layer of professional involvement, hiring a content editor to make a quick pass through the manuscript before the copy editor. This editor helps me sort out any lingering questions and alerts me to potential problems, but

---

* I use the terms "indie publishing" and "indie author" to refer to someone who self-publishes at a professional level, hiring a qualified team to help them produce books that sit comfortably alongside any traditionally-published book from the bookstore. It is still self-publishing, but with an emphasis on the highest possible quality.

she can do her work more quickly (and economically) because of the prior beta feedback process.

When to pay for an editor

If you plan to self-publish and you want people to pay for your books, it's a good idea to view your writing as a business. Many indie writers on a tight budget rely on a friend to check their books, then are disappointed when reviewers say things like: "Great story, but it's a shame about all the typos." Good editing is expensive, because it's time-consuming. An editor friend suggests writers put aside a little money each week from the time they start writing, to make it easier to afford good editing when the time comes.

If you are **seeking a traditional publisher**, you might choose to hire professionals at some stages, to bring out the best in your book and give it the greatest chance of being selected. If you're getting a lot of rejections that mention a writing problem you don't know how to resolve, a developmental or structural editor can help. And due to increasing pressure on the publishing industry, if your manuscript has a high number of typos and grammatical errors it might be passed over as "too hard" even if the content is good; a copy editor can help you make it more competitive.

Do experienced writers need feedback?

Yes. It's simply best practice to get the benefit of other opinions. The world's most accomplished writers work with editors, and many also seek beta feedback at various stages in their process.

Bestselling crime writer Rachel Amphlett (rachelamphlett.com) has more than twenty books to her name, but she remains a fan of beta readers. She says: "The hardest thing for me as a writer can be to accurately convey what's going on in my head into words. When I first started using beta readers, I provided them with a copy of the manuscript and a scope that set out what I needed from them. Through that process over a number of books, I can pre-empt the sort of issues they're going to raise and so I'm finding that I can sort a lot of those out during my own editing process before I hand over the manuscript to them. They'll still find phrases they don't understand (blame my quasi UK/Australian influences!), or places in a story where I haven't made myself clear, but it all helps with my writing process."

POWER TIP

Some people have told me beta feedback is a waste of time. I used to think perhaps they'd asked the wrong beta readers, but I've now realized there's a more empowering answer.

The key to successful beta feedback is much closer to home.

It is you!

You are the pivot point of your beta feedback process.

The results will depend on who you choose, how you brief them and empower them for their task, and how you sift through their feedback and choose your response.

This news might be a little confronting but is also encouraging. It gives us more control over the outcomes of the beta feedback process and greater possibilities for growth. If you don't like the results you're getting, think laterally—there might be a way.

The beta feedback we receive might be mundane or hostile or confusing or just plain wrong. That's okay, because we are not looking for people to tell us what to do and/or how to fix our manuscripts.

> **This is so important! We will be forever disappointed in our beta readers if we expect them to take over our role as captain of our own manuscripts.**

We are looking for people to tell us how the book made them feel and, if they possibly can, *why* it made them feel that way. We can then filter their conflicting reactions. External perspectives—when we reflect on them without bowing to them—help us get to know ourselves and our writing better. Growing self-knowledge empowers us as writers.

There's nothing wrong with making a few mistakes to start with. I muddled through my first attempts at beta feedback management and had to grow into the task. Take time to learn what works for you and your books. Find people who suit you, and figure out which types of feedback they excel at.

Everyone has a different superpower. Find people who can see what's in your blind spots so your vision can grow.

Incredible books and amazing writers blossom when the conditions are right. I've seen it again and again in the past twenty years. Beta readers and useful feedback have changed people's publishing careers. They've changed mine. They can change yours, too.

A quick recap

- The beta version of your manuscript is the test version.
- A beta reader is like a test pilot, or a mirror that helps you see yourself and your writing differently.
- A beta reader is *not* an editor, leader, guide or fixer, and you must retain control of your manuscript, vision and voice.
- A successful beta feedback process centers on you: who you choose, how you brief them, and how you respond to their feedback.

Chapter 3. The ideal beta reader

Is there one ideal beta reader? Maybe a book editor, an English teacher, or an award-winning, bestselling author?

No, there isn't one ideal beta reader. In fact, any of the people I just mentioned might turn out not to be very good at beta reading—or they may be a good beta reader, but not the right one for you.

There will be a set of ideal beta reader characteristics for *your* book and the way you work. It's a unique set. Use this chapter not as a checklist, but as an identikit for you to build up a picture of what could be most useful to you.

You will never find a person who exemplifies all your ideal beta reader attributes, but across a team of beta readers you might cover most of them.

In this chapter...

- Demographics of the ideal beta reader.
- Personality traits and relevant experience.
- Reading and writing characteristics to look for.
- How much publishing knowledge should a beta reader have?

A note about choosing

Some people have great results from random beta reader connections, but others don't. I personally have found a more strategic approach gives me better results. Therefore, in this book I will focus on ways to build a team of people you know and trust, who have useful and complementary skills.

> Louise* says: "Except for one friend, I have blindly taken readers from the internet and I wish there was a better way to screen them. You are asking a tremendous favor from these people—to spend time and trouble reading your work and also make intelligent comments about it."

> True crime author Garry Rodgers (dyingwords.net) says: "I had someone offer to beta read. They came back with a bizarre and vulgar response. I don't think it was a troll—just a nutcase. My takeaway was to vet beta readers before sending them the manuscript."

Demographics

Look for someone who is in the target audience for your book, in terms of age, gender, interests, education level, socio-economic status and so on. This person will naturally respond to your book in a similar way to the intended reader, without having to think about it.

---

* "Louise," like the other authors in this book who are mentioned only by a first name, was a respondent to my survey about beta feedback who gave permission for comments to be used anonymously. Names are changed for privacy purposes.

Chapter 3. The ideal beta reader

- Writing a children's book? Make sure you have at least some child beta readers in the right age group. (They will tend to be brutally honest, so brace yourself!) Parents, grandparents, school teachers and babysitters also read children's books, and are often the ones who buy the books. Their feedback will be useful.
- Writing a book on nuclear fission for university students? You need some university students among your beta readers—preferably several of varying academic ability, so that the A-grade students know whether you've got it right, and the ones who struggle can tell you whether the explanations helped them.

Not sure who your target reader is? That's a common problem. Few of us know it when we start writing, and even once we've figured it out, it is often refined or even redirected over time.

A few tips:

- Are you deliberately writing the kind of book you like to read? Your target reader is **you**. List your own characteristics such as age, gender, occupation and interests as if you were a stranger, then look for some beta readers who match.
- Do you have anyone in mind as you write? This is often particularly relevant for types of non-fiction, but can apply to any genre. For example, I met a man who wrote a business book hoping it would help his teenage son. If you do have a person in mind, imagine them and develop a list of demographics. Do some research if necessary.
- Do you have readers who are already especially interested in your work? If there's lots of them, do a survey via your website or email list, using a tool like Google forms. They

might be happy to answer questions about their interests that help you develop a sense of what they have in common as a group. If there's only a few, maybe you can ask them directly—even in person if appropriate.

Personality and experience

Look for someone who is neither too gentle nor too harsh, and whose personality or experience has helped them develop a type of discernment that allows them to see possibilities.

- **Can they put themselves in a hypothetical reader's shoes?** Can they see the strengths of something that may not appeal to them personally?
- **Ideally, they know what they think and aren't afraid to say so**, but can express their opinions without killing your dreams. They can criticize in a way that makes you hopeful about what you could do to fix it rather than sinking you into despair. However, if you have to choose between "too brutal" and "too kind," you're probably better to go for the more painful option because you really do need to hear the truth. (Consider fortifying yourself with chocolate or comfort food of choice before reading their report. Then give yourself a day or two to recover before you start taking action.)
- **They are not so close to you that they will find it hard to say things you don't want to hear.** Some friends are able to speak honestly from the heart, but others will hold back—they value the relationship more than your book. This was a key problem identified in my survey (see Chapter 1). Does the connection you have with them allow honesty without damaging the relationship?

- **Usually, they are not your mother or life partner.** Yes, this is a bother, because that was someone you could have asked! Some people find it creates friction at home if they ask their partner. Others find loved ones can't read with fresh eyes because they are putting it through the filter of all the things they've ever heard you say, and comparing even a fictional manuscript to events or relationships they know about from your past. There are always exceptions to this; some close relatives can stand back and give you an objective perspective.

> Bestselling crime writer Rachel Amphlett (rachelamphlett.com) says: "All four of my beta readers are family and friends, but what's important is that they're avid readers of the genre I write, so they know the tropes and have high expectations. They also don't pull any punches if they find something that doesn't make sense!"

Reading and writing characteristics

Look for people who read often, and possibly also enjoy writing. If you've been to their house, it probably has bookshelves in places where you can see them, or they always have an e-reader nearby. Maybe they often mention a book they've read.

- **Ideally, they read broadly**—neither a book snob who only reads impenetrable "literature," nor someone who never reads anything other than short mass-market novels. A good mix of popular and literary reading, as well as an interest in both fiction and non-fiction, will give them a broad perspective which enriches their beta feedback.

- If the target audience for your book is people who don't read much, you might deliberately seek one or two beta readers with that characteristic, just to check if the book is working for them.

> One of my editing clients, Ian "Watto" Watson of Shed Happens, writes encouraging books for "the 78% of men who never read a book" (his own tongue-in-cheek statistic). Why would he publish for people who don't read for pleasure? Because it helps him reach more people than he can meet face to face, and will continue to do so even after he has retired from his speaking career. He might only address a particular men's group for a day, but his books continue to speak to those men and others for months, years or decades. We typeset the book in larger print with more white space between lines, divided the page with shaded boxes, and formatted several key sentences in bold on each page. We sent it to more than 20 beta readers in the target demographic, testing not just the words but the layout. Most responses were brief—that was fine, because we weren't looking for the usual detailed beta report. When several of them said: "I couldn't put it down," we knew we'd found a solution that could work.

- **They are often (but not always) writers themselves**, because fellow writers understand the challenges of creating a book-length manuscript in a way that no one else can. They are also less likely to get fixated on that dangling modifier on page 214, because they know that's only a tiny part of what makes a writer. Fellow writers are also motivated to help you with your book, because

they know they're going to need a beta reader soon. They comprehend the value of useful beta feedback.
- **Some authors prefer to avoid asking fellow writers.** They want someone whose reaction is uninfluenced by various writerly presuppositions and agonizing over writing craft. If you're not sure yet what you prefer, I suggest trialling a mix of writers and non-writers.

> Award-winning literary author Orna Ross (ornaross.com) offers another perspective: "I prefer beta readers who have nothing to do with writing or publishing but are avid readers in the particular genre. In my opinion, they need to be an unusual mix of general reader with an acute sense of what does or doesn't work for them about a piece of writing." She has built an effective beta team this way.

- **Ideally, they have never read your manuscript before.** Fresh eyes will give you the best value from beta feedback, giving you the kind of untainted response that you'd get from a person picking up your book in a store. Try to have at least one beta reader who knows nothing about the book beforehand.
- Someone who only ever reads sports biographies won't be the best judge of a paranormal-romance-thriller and vice versa. **Someone who reads your genre—often and by choice**—will be familiar with the way such books tend to be structured, without even having to think about it. They will have an instinct for what works and doesn't work. They will recognize where you have broken established rules, and be more likely to evaluate wisely whether or not you've gotten away with it.

- **On the other hand, sometimes a reader of other genres can give you ideas that deepen your book.** You will need to weigh their feedback, being wary of suggestions that might lead you away from important genre expectations, but balancing this against other ideas that trigger a spark of brilliance.

> A couple of my beta readers for my light memoir were experienced in more dramatic or traumatic types of memoir. They opened my mind to ways I could keep it light and yet add a deeper undercurrent to the narrative.

Publishing smarts

People who are savvy about publishing issues are handy to have on your team. They don't need to have worked in the publishing industry; they might just be people who pay attention to the finer points of the books they read, or keep up with blogs and articles about writing and publishing.

- **Ideal beta readers understand what makes a good book** in terms of things like plot development and characterization, structure and purpose. They understand what creates suspense, and what draws a reader to keep on reading till the end. They recognize what creates a good resolution and what falls flat.
- In a non-fiction book, they comprehend the value of **theme** and a cohesive structure. They can recognize whether your central message builds logically or not.
- **They recognize the difference between what your school teachers told you was Proper Writing, and what represents a writer's "voice."** They are not afraid to deviate

from "technically correct" if there is something that actually works better, and communicates more effectively. They can weigh up your eccentricities as a writer, and give you an opinion on which ones are making your book come alive versus the ones that you probably should ditch because they're clunky or obstructive.

- **They understand what is relatively unimportant in a first beta read.** I've seen manuscripts and writers receive devastating feedback because of a few typos, because the beta reader had never seen a book-in-progress before. I'm not suggesting we don't try to be accurate as writers, just that a good beta reader understands that a few typos will happen, no matter how good a writer is, and there are bigger issues to look at in deciding whether or not a book "works."

- **If your book is in a specialist field, they have knowledge and experience in that field,** or at least a strong interest in it. For example, if your book is about nuclear medicine, you probably want a beta reader who knows something about nuclear medicine. If on the other hand, your book is *Nuclear Medicine for Newbies*, you'll want at least one beta reader who knows nuclear medicine (to make sure you've got the science right) and another beta reader who doesn't know nuclear medicine (to make sure you have adequately explained it for a non-expert).

Memoir author Jane says: "I was lucky that my beta reader had had an emotional life-changing experience and could relate to the emotions I aroused in my writing. She put a lot of effort into her critique."

- **If your book is set in a particular location, it can be handy to have a beta reader who knows the location well,** so they can tell you what doesn't ring true. A reader who knows nothing about the location can tell you if the location came alive in their minds. If you can't have both, weigh up which matters more for your book. For example, in non-fiction, accuracy might be more important, whereas in a novel it might be more important to have built a believable world.
- Ideally, they are savvy about the publishing world and have **good instincts about what it takes to get a book noticed by a literary agent or a book buyer.** They are familiar enough with the state of publishing to know that self-publishing is no longer the poor cousin, and traditional publishing is in a state of flux. They understand at some level what makes a person buy a book in a store versus on the internet. They often know the latest books that have been successful, but they don't think aping those books is the only way for you to succeed, or even the best way for you to succeed.

Case study: How I chose a team

This is how I chose my beta feedback team for *Dogged Optimism*, a light memoir about a dog. The team was custom-built for the project, and included some beta readers I hadn't used for other books.

The manuscript began as a series of amusing anecdotes about the dog's various catastrophes, but as I wrote, it became deeper and broader—my story as well as the dog's. I couldn't find a way to avoid mentioning events such as the sudden death of my father. I wrestled with how to include bleak moments in a mostly-humorous book. I was eager for feedback as to whether I was going too far/not far enough with those elements.

It's also a particularly Australian story, full of the way Australians live and the things we talk about—and some of our dangerous wildlife. I needed international feedback so that my book could retain its "Down Under" flavor without becoming unintelligible to people from other countries.

I had big issues to discuss, and a very tight timeframe, so I assembled a bigger team than I might otherwise have done:

- To give me a greater cross-section of opinions on the controversial topics. This helps even out bias.
- So that I had backup in case they couldn't all respond within the tight timeframe.

The six people I invited had similarities and differences.

Similarities:

- All were pet lovers. Anyone who doesn't like animals is likely to find *Dogged Optimism* puzzling or irritating.
- All were interested in personal growth, and could evaluate whether or not the manuscript was encouraging.
- All were interested in reading, writing and publishing.

Differences:

- They were of diverse nationalities—two Aussies, two Americans, one Canadian and one Brit.
- They were from different walks of life. Three were people I met on Twitter and then got to know over time as we commented on each other's blogs. The other three were friends from my work, my travels and my public speaking club.

- They had been in my life for various amounts of time—from two to twenty years.

It turned out to be one of my most useful beta feedback experiences.

POWER TIP

When you read the list of desirable characteristics in this chapter, were there some you wanted to dismiss, or which even repelled you? It's possible this reaction is alerting you to characteristics you lack. It can be powerful to have some beta readers who are our polar opposites, for example:

- If you're a detail person, look for someone who's better at big-picture thinking.
- If you're not good at grammar or you don't think it's very important, include a beta reader who loves it.
- If you spend your work life writing formal reports, balance your feedback by including a beta reader skilled in much more informal types of writing.

Know your strengths. Identify the opposite of those strengths, and look for someone who has them. You might find it useful to draw up a table listing and comparing your own strengths to those of your beta readers.

Sometimes, the feedback from these "balance beta readers" is the most irritating and hard to accept of our various beta reports. Just take your time, let it settle, and think about it from every angle. You might not do exactly what they suggest, but you might attend to the issues they raise in a different way. More on this in Chapter 9.

A quick recap

- Look for at least some beta readers who match the demographics of your target audience.
- Ideal beta readers:
  - » Know what they think and can articulate this, without being cruel or disheartening.
  - » Read often and widely, and at least some of them are fans of the genre you are writing.
  - » Understand the current world of publishing well enough to know what makes a good book for today's readers.
  - » Can look beyond errors that are not important at this phase of your process to see what really matters to your book.
- If you are in a rush and need to ensure you get at least some feedback in time, or if you have a particularly vexing issue and need multiple perspectives to sort it out, consider inviting a bigger team.
- Look for people who can fill the gaps of your knowledge or personality, and don't necessarily avoid getting opinions from beta readers who irritate you—it might be a sign that they can supply what you lack.

Chapter 4. Where to find the right beta readers for you

A LOT OF MY BLOG READERS and workshop participants hope I will reveal a magic website or Facebook forum where they can go this afternoon and engage a dozen beta readers perfect for their project.

As I look back over the past seven years since I began seriously seeking beta feedback, I see that my team has grown much more organically than that, through the development of human connection and friendship. I appreciate the results that have emerged from this approach, and not just in terms of manuscript improvement. Writing can be a lonely profession, but I'm now surrounded by people who make me feel supported and inspired—people I trust to be part of my writing career for years to come.

May I encourage you to try to get at least some of your beta readers in this slower, more relational way? In this chapter, I'll explain what has worked for me and others, so that you can borrow whatever is useful to you. As always, no rules.

In this chapter...

- How to network with other writers to find people who are a good match for your writing style and might enjoy helping you.
- How to find specialists in a particular topic.

- Where to look for beta readers who are *not* writers.
- When to start looking.

Connecting with other writers

A few years ago, I knew only a couple of writers other than the ones I encountered in my work as an editor. Now I seem to know dozens of them. Some have become great friends.

A bond seems to form between writers. Whenever I meet a fellow writer for coffee, especially another indie author, we talk at a thousand miles an hour about all things books and publishing, as though there's just not enough oxygen for all the talk. I've had this happen multiple times with people of different personalities. Often, we're still calling out more ideas across the widening gap as we walk to our separate cars. These connections nourish me as a writer and as a human.

These networks have also provided quite a few of my beta readers.

Connections started happening for me after I began making more of an effort to go where other writers go—both physical places and online—and to talk to others when I got there. Some days I find it hard to talk to strangers, but I found that the more I did it, the easier it became.

POWER TIP

This might sound obvious to you, but from many of my conversations I know that it's not obvious to lots of writers: don't start by looking for beta readers. Start by connecting, sharing interests, and encouraging one another. Wait a while before you broach the subject of beta reading.

Meeting other writers in person

Writing seminars, workshops and conferences
I love attending workshops and conferences to learn, but I now also make an effort to chat with other writers in the breaks.

Local writers' groups
In my city these can often be found listed in libraries or on library websites. Some are connected with writers' centers. If you Google [writers group] and the name of your location, you might get some options near you.

POWER TIP

Try attending writers' events and groups on your own instead of going with a friend. For me, it feels a little intimidating to go alone, and yet I seem to meet a lot more people. When I go with a friend, I tend to get engrossed in talking to that person; when I go on my own, I'm more likely to notice others.

I find that social media helps expand connections. Following each other on Twitter or checking out each other's blogs feels less intense than asking for a phone number or email address.

I've seen some connections grow into friendship while others fade gently. And some have bloomed in later months or years. The more connections I have, the more relaxed I am about letting it happen or not happen.

A fellow author attended one of my workshops. When I saw her a couple of months later at a writers' event, I casually asked if she'd like to beta for me. It was more off-the-cuff than my usual requests, and yet I did already know she was interested in the topic of my book. She said yes, and gave me valuable beta feedback.

Meeting other writers online

Real people are behind social media shares and blog posts. If you get to know their interests and writing styles it can help you decide if the two of you might be a good match as fellow beta readers.

Twitter

I have found Twitter to be a powerful social network for meeting other writers. Several of my favorite beta readers, career supporters, and true friends are people I met on Twitter. We began by replying, commenting and retweeting each other's posts on Twitter, expanded beyond Twitter to comment on each other's blogs, and in time some of these friendships developed to the point of email or Skype conversations, or meeting in person.

Facebook

Search for Facebook groups for writers in your specialty. Take an interest in other people's posts, and make helpful comments that reveal your character and interests. Pay attention to the character and interests revealed by others, and what resonates with you.

Other social platforms

Check out the presence of writers on your social network of choice. Even LinkedIn has a lot of writing and publishing groups.

Don't let geography stop you. There are large oceans between me and several of my beta readers. In fact, one of the strengths of my team is that they can give feedback on communication issues related to writing for a global audience.

Visiting writing blogs

I found that as I commented on people's blog articles, over time they visited my blog and commented there. Friendships developed from those beginnings, especially when we shared values and interests. Sometimes, I also got to know a blogger's regular commenters.

> On Twitter, I met a fellow editor. We visited each other's blogs. We had similar views about where publishing was heading. After many months, I offered to pay her for a manuscript assessment, but she preferred to exchange free beta reads.

> A favorite blogger I met on Twitter was writing a memoir. I contacted her via her website and offered to beta read for her, as I love the way she writes and have edited quite a few memoirs. A year later, she returned the favor.

> When I tweeted about a manuscript deadline, I got a "how can I help?" tweet from a blogger I follow. We both write mysteries and appreciate each other's sense of humor. I was hesitant to ask for beta feedback, but I took the plunge. She has been one of my star beta readers for years now. I enjoy critiquing her manuscripts in return.

> Jodie says: "My beta reader gave me alternative ways of looking at my non-fiction book. She commented on things that she really liked as well as areas that needed clarification, refining or reworking. Though I have never met her in person, I feel that she has become a good friend through the process."

POWER TIP

It can be hard to find time to blog, but one of the less discussed benefits of blogging is the chance to meet other writers. You can be yourself on your own blog. People can get to know you better there, away from the clutter and noise of social platforms.

Friends and family

In Chapter 3, I said it's often not a good idea to ask your mother or your spouse, but sometimes they can be exactly the right person. It all depends on the person, the relationship and the book.

Sometimes, friends show genuine interest in your manuscript and ask detailed questions. They're often the people who will be savvy enough to give good feedback, and are likely to enjoy the process. Sometimes we overlook them because they are right in front of us.

 A long-time friend in another country had been asking deep questions about how my novel was progressing and I thought: why not ask? She was excited to help, gave valuable feedback, and has continued to take a close interest in my books.

 Another friend declined giving feedback on a crime novel but said: "I'll definitely critique your dog book."

 My mother is great at keeping it short. I, on the other hand, am not. My first draft of one book was about 20,000 words overweight, and I struggled to decide what to cut. I gave Mum a printout and asked her to put a red line through anything that didn't need to be there. She was hesitant to hurt my feelings at first, and it looked like it wasn't going to work. Then I assured her: "I'd rather hear it from you now than bad reviews later." Once she got into her stride it became a red pen festival—sometimes with cheeky comments in the margin that made me laugh out loud. She has given me usefully-brutal feedback on every manuscript since.

Finding specialist beta readers

Sometimes a book needs a specialist check, a sensitivity reader, or people who are squarely in the target readership. You'll never please everybody, but some checking is definitely worthwhile—for your own credibility, to avoid spreading harmful misconceptions, and for the sake of readers who sometimes feel marginalized by misleading portrayals.

I use my old journalism instincts to track down people I could ask. See whether the following suggestions trigger ideas for how to find your own specialists.

- **Sports, fitness, endurance, extreme sports**: try asking members of a local team or club, yoga or aerobics instructors, nutritionists, sports fans, running group participants, gym members and attendees, people who sell fitness or nutrition products to these people and might be expected to know their market, tourism operators who service the market.
- **Business, investing, entrepreneurship, public speaking**: try local business associations, speaking clubs, service clubs such as Rotary, recruitment consultants, teachers of adult education in relevant fields, business mentoring groups, government departments set up to assist business planning, fellow writers who own businesses.
- **Cookbooks, food, wine**: look for people who attend or present cookery classes, school teachers who teach about food preparation, nutritionists, caterers, people who work in specialist homewares stores, owners or staff of cafes and restaurants, vintners, home brewers.
- **Arts, music, theatre, photography**: consider asking university lecturers in particular specialties, adult educators, interest clubs, art gallery owners or curators, professional artists or photographers, musicians, music teachers, music store owners or staff, drama teachers, actors, producers, directors, bloggers or Instagrammers who have an obvious interest in the area, researchers, school teachers.

- **Remote or rural life**: approach writers' groups located in the relevant region, tourism authorities for the relevant region, bloggers and Instagrammers who live in and post about life in the places you write about, tourism operators who go into your destination and know it well.
- **History**: you might find help from museum staff with relevant qualifications, university lecturers, school teachers with a specialty, local history clubs and committees.
- **Sciences, engineering, space travel, information technology, sci-fi**: try university lecturers and students in the particular field, researchers who post their findings online and in a form that general readers can understand (because they might be more likely to want to help, and to have the ability to help), writers who happen to work in a relevant field regardless of what they write about—find them on social networks.
- **Religion, spirituality**: consider asking ministers or leaders in the relevant religion, people who blog or post on social media about similar topics, lecturers or students at religious colleges, people who run applicable events or conferences.
- **Teen and young adult**: potential teen beta readers might include members of youth groups, children of friends, young adults who were recently teens. Adult "youth specialists" might include community or church youth leaders, social workers, librarians, school teachers, parents of teens, government or private youth workers, fellow writers who have children in the right age group.
- **Children's books**: child beta readers might include your own children or their friends or classmates, children of friends, the children of writers you know. Adult beta readers might include school teachers, Sunday School

teachers, parents of children in the age group, babysitters, fitness and dance instructors, friends who love to read to their children, fellow writers with children.

Think laterally
Think carefully about what you need to know, then think laterally to imagine who might happen to know it. See if a quick online search about the topic sparks any unusual ideas for where to find specialists. Ask friends who they know.

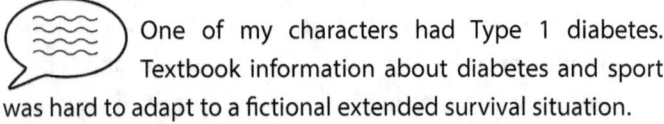 One of my characters had Type 1 diabetes. Textbook information about diabetes and sport was hard to adapt to a fictional extended survival situation.

- On Twitter, I met a writer who was also a nurse. I asked her if she knew anyone who could help me, and she offered to Skype with me herself. She discussed key considerations and over the video connection showed me how a blood glucose monitor worked.

- Via Twitter and blogs, I encountered a journalist and author who had family members with Type 1 diabetes. I didn't know her very well, but because she was an outspoken advocate for research I decided to be bold and contact her via her website. I asked if she would consider checking purely the diabetes elements of the plot. I also tried to make it as easy as possible for her to say no. She said yes! And oh my, did I need that check. She gave me what the textbooks couldn't tell me. The diabetes storyline is now dramatically different as a result of her detailed feedback. We have since become beta buddies, exchanging beta reads on multiple manuscripts.

> I visited a small town to interview police. Later in the writing process I discovered more things I needed to know. I tried several avenues, but no one was returning my calls or emails—it's one thing to stand in a small-town police station looking nerdy and harmless and ask politely about weaponry; it's quite another to ask from the anonymity of a phone call or email! I searched online for a police manuscript consultant without success, but in the process stumbled upon a retired police inspector who had written a book on an unrelated topic. I made a tentative approach via his website. He agreed to do the check for me! I isolated the sections of my manuscript that included police procedures, so that he didn't have to read the whole thing. He gave me incredibly valuable feedback—not just corrections but suggestions for how to get around plot problems related to procedure. He even improved the characterization of my police officers.

> For a book set on the Great Barrier Reef, many hours of research had failed to produce a convincing motivation for my villain. I attended a presentation at a writers' festival by a Reef historian. Afterwards, I was first in line at the book signing table. I said I was writing a crime novel and could I ask a question. Instead of being annoyed or offended, this distinguished academic almost rubbed his hands together with glee, saying: "I always hope I'll get one of these!" His answers to my questions set off a fireworks display in my synapses. (I can't share it here, alas—it's a spoiler.) He also gave me an email introduction to a relevant expert.

POWER TIPS

If you are nervous about approaching a specialist, don't assume they won't want to do it. My motto is: you never know if you don't ask. If you approach them in a respectful way, there is always a chance they will say yes.

- I've found that a specialist or sensitivity reader who is somehow connected to writing or publishing is often more open to helping, because they understand why we need it. Sometimes they will even think it sounds like a fun thing to do.

- Always remember that every specialist is also a human being with relationships and interests. You might know a specialist already and not realize it. Maybe there's a rocket scientist among the other parents you chat to every week while you wait outside your child's art class. If you include your writing in the conversation, sometimes helpful connections emerge.

- Specialists can be passionate about their topic. Sometimes, our errors raise strong emotions for them. If you stand back and evaluate the feedback carefully—even when it's hard to hear—it can bless your manuscript and your writing career.

- Children can be brutal in their feedback, and will often simply refuse to finish a book they don't like. This doesn't necessarily mean no one will like it. Try to invite at least five or six to beta read, so that you have a more balanced outcome—and consider allowing time for a second round of beta readers if necessary.

Other ways to recruit beta readers

Contests
Some reputable writing competitions have manuscript development as part of the prize. Try Googling [manuscript development feedback critique competition contest] and see what comes up that is near to you, or at least in your country. Many writers' associations also send regular email alerts about upcoming competitions.

> I won a contest that included several meetings with a manuscript consultant. She read my manuscript at different stages, and it was a great way for me to overcome my early reluctance to have anyone read something that wasn't yet "perfect."

Large teams
Some authors find it powerful to use a large beta testing team, most often recruited via their email subscriber list or using a sign-up form on their website.

> Bestselling fantasy author Michael Wisehart (michaelwisehart.com) says: "The first book in my epic fantasy series went through three different rounds of testing with nearly 100 readers of all ages, races and sexes—very diverse. My books in that series are between 600-700 pages, so I need to make sure all the storylines make sense. I sent out a very clear instruction sheet, so they understood what I was looking for. Their feedback gave me great perspective

from many vantage points. My book wouldn't be what it is today without them."

I know other authors who also have 30 or more beta testers and have developed an effective process.

However, be aware that a large team is not right for everyone. I have seen authors get too much feedback, struggle to make sense of all the conflicting opinions, and lose traction—or even worse, lose their vision for their own book.

Personally, I prefer to engage at a deep level with a smaller, hand-selected team, and so that is the type of beta feedback process I focus on in this book. If you sense that the larger team might be right for you, go for it! Test, observe and adjust your system, until you have a method that works for you and your books.

Attitudes that help

- **Be real.** Try to avoid "casing" people to see if they might make a good beta reader before you bother getting to know them. Make friends with people you actually like! It's much better in the long run.
- **Be patient.** I knew some Twitter friends for a year before we asked each other for beta feedback.
- **Be generous.** Help people if you have the skill and the time, even if they may never be able to help you.
- **Be relaxed.** Some people won't want to get to know you better, and that's okay. Some people do want to know you, but don't want to be your beta reader. It doesn't mean the next person won't want to do so.

When to look

If you want to use the friendship model for building a beta feedback team, be aware that it takes time. It's a good idea to start looking now for the beta readers you need in six months or a year. Sometimes you'll find the right beta readers quickly, but please don't rely on it.

POWER TIPS

We often want to ask for tips from the writers we most admire. However, a famous multi-published author with whom you have no personal connection will probably not have the time or the desire to beta read your book. It's not that they don't respect you or wish you well. It's just that they probably get a hundred such requests every week and turn them all down as a matter of policy.

- Your requests will often meet with more success if you invite people who are at a similar stage in their writing career.
- Sometimes, insight comes from an unexpected quarter. I'm selective about who I choose as beta readers, but I've also taken a risk sometimes on a person who didn't seem particularly skilled or qualified. Their ideas have sparked great improvements.

Fantasy/thriller writer Judy L. Mohr (judylmohr.com) says: "I have had awesome feedback from a new writer. She wasn't able to give suggestions to fix the issues she found, but she was able to describe why a passage wasn't working for her. That's what makes great feedback."

A quick recap

- Use social media platforms and blogs to get to know and like people who share similar interests.
- Attend writers' events and talk to people during the coffee breaks.
- Think ahead. It takes time to get to know and trust people.
- Try to build genuine two-way connections, rather than just approaching people out of the blue to ask for a favor. You might feel like you know them, but do they know you?
- When people show genuine interest in your book project, pay attention.
- Pay it forward—if you have time, offer to beta read for others, even if they're not going to return the favor any time soon.
- You don't know if you don't ask.

PART 2:
Managing the feedback process for your book

When to engage beta readers during the writing process, how to build a relationship with them, and tips for preparing an effective briefing document.

Chapter 5. When to use beta readers

Let's look at how beta readers might fit into the different steps of the path from blank page to published book. What tasks could you give them at each stage?

As always, these are not rules. Trial them, then tweak them to build a workflow customized to your goals, situation and personality.

In this chapter...

- Where beta readers can add value in each phase of creating a book, complementing tasks a professional editor might do.
- When to use or avoid beta readers, depending on your goals and level of experience.
- Whether to engage your beta team all at once, or spread them out over the project timeline.

Flowchart: Seven phases of feedback

Download a full-size free copy of the following flowchart at usefulwritingtips.com, where you will also find other useful resources for writers and beta readers.

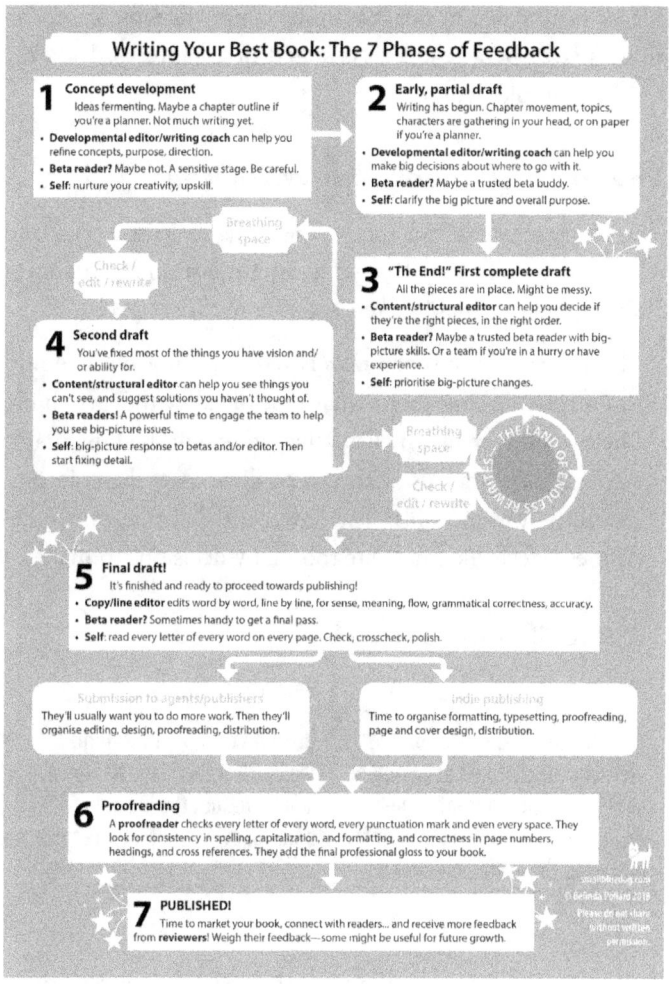

The phases of publishing

Professional editors perform different tasks in different stages of the publishing process. I integrate beta feedback with my editorial workflow by varying the timing of my requests to beta readers, and the type of feedback I ask of them at different phases.

Please note that I'm not recommending you replace professionals with beta readers. As stated in Chapter 2, I see the tasks as complementary.

Phase 1: Concept development

This is where you decide that you're going to write a book and what it will be about. This phase might last an afternoon or twenty years. (It took me ten years on my first novel.)

> **Imagine:** The author's task is like standing on a mountaintop, thinking about what type of valley they will build below. How many towns? What work will the inhabitants do? Which way does the river flow? Are there forests, swamps, or sand hills? The power is delightful, but sometimes it feels like there are too many decisions to make.

IDEAL FEEDBACK IN PHASE 1	
Professional	Beta reader
Developmental editor or writing coach: looks at an outline or discusses the concept, to help an author decide what's in or out, and what the overall purpose is.	Use with caution! The wrong feedback at this stage has been known to suck the life out of a book, or even make a writer give up.

Fiction
- I'm incredibly wary about beta feedback at this sensitive stage, especially for new writers. I've seen great ideas abandoned because a writer got early feedback from the wrong person and lost confidence.
- If you really do want concept feedback, choose a highly-trusted and preferably experienced person. Prepare yourself to untangle confusing and often dispiriting

feedback. It's a rare beta reader who can foresee what an unformed idea can become.

- Consider getting incidental feedback instead of a formal beta report. Prepare an "elevator pitch" which sums up your story in one to three sentences. Practice telling it to people, and see how they react. If they're not interested, is it the wrong idea, or just the wrong reader? Yes, it's a labyrinth of possibilities, but writers grow when they learn to interpret reactions. Test and tweak the pitch, to see how the reactions change.

Memoir

- As you tell your life stories to people, see what clicks with them. We all have "scripts" we use for those stories we tell all the time. Tweak them each time, and see how reactions change.

- Pay attention to the follow-up questions people ask, and think about how you could answer those questions in the manuscript, and which you might leave hanging. This early "market testing" is telling you what to include in your memoir and how to frame it.

Non-fiction

- Consider showing your outline to a specialist in the field you are writing about. What do they think of what you're including, what you're leaving out, and the order you've proposed?

- I've seen non-fiction writers ask their blog readership for feedback on aspects of their upcoming book. This has the added benefit of alerting their online communities that a book they might like is coming soon.

> While writing this book, I presented webinars and face-to-face workshops. My feedback forms from participants represented another type of beta feedback. Each time I prepared to speak I tweaked the presentation accordingly, and then got more feedback from the new audience. If you're a speaker, consider trying a similar process with your non-fiction topic.

Phase 2: Early, partial draft

You've actually got a few chapters written now, or perhaps 20–30,000 words of a full-length novel.

Imagine: The basic framework of the author's "valley" is in place, but perhaps they are still deciding between features. If they are a "discovery writer" or "pantser" (one who writes "by the seat of their pants"), they might prefer to discover their valley on the ground, experiencing one feature at a time and realizing what they want it to do. Sometimes, they'd like another opinion to help them decide.

IDEAL FEEDBACK IN PHASE 2	
Professional	Beta reader
Developmental editor or writing coach: looks at various materials such as a chapter outline or synopsis, character lists, sample chapters; opens your eyes to pervasive or consistent flaws and suggests remedies; helps you work out where you are headed, what to include/exclude.	I don't recommend a beta team yet, but some people (including me) do interact with a beta buddy at this stage. Be wise, and only use someone whose character and opinions you trust.

- Consider developing a partnership with a "beta buddy" you trust, especially if you're trying something new. I'd lean towards discussing ideas rather than giving them anything to read. Everyone works differently, however, so develop a process that suits you.
- Be careful who you choose. First, I would want to be confident that their feedback will be useful and sensitive. Second, I'd want to know them well enough to trust their honesty. I don't want someone else writing my book before I can.
- Look for someone who can see the big picture and discipline themselves not to fixate on detail. Correcting commas is a waste of time at this point.
- The value of seeking feedback this early is that it can help reduce the amount of time you need to spend rewriting.
- The danger of seeking feedback this early is that it can shift you off-course if you are not confident enough in your vision.

I once received early feedback from a manuscript consultant. She asked what my "metanarrative" was—the book's overarching message. I made a quick guess (greed), but when the real metanarrative (forgiveness, and what happens when it's withheld) began to emerge later, I was able to recognize it and strengthen it because she had alerted me. This was professional feedback, but nevertheless it shows the type of big-picture issues that can benefit from early feedback.

Chapter 5. When to use beta readers

Phase 3: First complete draft

This is that glorious moment when you type "The End." (In reality you are just beginning, but celebrate anyway.)

Imagine: The author stands on the mountaintop viewing the beautiful valley they've created. Are those towns connected in the best way? Do they need to erase that toxic waste dump or plant a forest? Time for redevelopment.

IDEAL FEEDBACK IN PHASE 3	
Professional	Beta reader
Structure and content editor: shows you detailed possibilities for rearranging your book to be the strongest it can be, with comprehensive suggestions; sometimes does the work for you while making sure it still sounds like you. **Writing coach**: helps you find out what you want it to become and empowers you to do it yourself.	Needs to be a person who can see past typos to the big picture. If you or your readers are inexperienced, it can be better to wait till the more polished second draft, so that there are less distractions.

I've noticed it's often better to wait to engage the full beta team until the more polished second draft, after your first big self-edit/rewrite. The manuscript is more polished, making it easier for inexperienced beta readers to see the value of what you've written. You are also more confident in what your book is about, and less likely to give up because of a poorly-worded or ill-conceived criticism.

If you are on a deadline crunch, however, you might need to engage your beta readers now. Some thoughts:

- Ask for big-picture feedback, not detail corrections. You're going to rearrange all your pieces, probably delete whole sections, and add a lot more typos before you're finished.

- Inexperienced beta readers might obsess over typos even though you ask them not to. Be prepared for the fact that sometimes they make judgments as a result. Authors have been told that a book full of light and magic is no good because they didn't punctuate dialogue correctly. Grammar and typos can be fixed; grammar can also be learned. Storytelling DNA is a whole other precious thing that should be nurtured.

> With two of my books, I was on such a tight deadline that I sent out a first draft. In the first case, some of my beta readers had trouble seeing the possibilities. I felt dejected and lost traction for a while, perhaps because as a memoir it was so personal. The second was a non-fiction book and I didn't feel the same emotional burden, but it made the task less enjoyable for my beta readers, and also meant that I missed out on higher-level feedback they might have been able to offer on a more complete manuscript. Reworking your manuscript before sending it to beta readers—whenever possible—honors your beta readers, gets you deeper results, and sometimes avoids emotional kryptonite for yourself.

```
Interlude: Breathing space
```
Whether you have beta feedback to respond to or as yet just your own perspective, you need fresh eyes to see your manuscript's flaws and possibilities. We get fresh eyes through **distance**.

Use time, if you have that luxury. Anywhere between a week and a year is good. (Maybe not ten years, though.)

If you are on a strict deadline and must get back to it soon, try these ideas:

- Shift to another space—work in a library, a cafe, the beach or even just a different room.
- Focus your mind on other topics—go for a walk, read something completely different, watch a movie, meet a friend for coffee.

Remember the view from the mountaintop? It needs distance or in the case of this illustration, height, to see where all the pieces go. Give yourself space to find new and creative ways to resolve the issues raised, and the energy to tackle it.

As we'll discuss further in Chapter 9, some of us are relaxed about beta feedback, and some find it unsettling or even devastating. With distance, however, a criticism that really stung takes on a new perspective. Either it recedes and you can see that it's not right for you, or you can see that it *is* right for you and you can roll up your sleeves and do something about it. The more personal the manuscript, the more you may need to be kind to yourself at this point.

Work time: Check/edit/rewrite

Prepare yourself; rewriting a book is a big job. When I was rewriting a first draft of 110,000 words, I compared it to teaching Latin dancing to a blue whale.

There is more in Chapter 9 about how to make the most of your rewrites, but for now, may I give you a couple of tips from an old editor:

- Don't be afraid to pull your manuscript to pieces and put it back together again. It will survive and so will you.

- Try to allow at least a few weeks for responding to any beta feedback before submitting to your editor if you possibly can. The more time you allow, the more value you'll get from the process.
- Consider making big-picture changes to the manuscript first, and then making another pass to sort out the detail. (More on this in Chapter 9.)
- It's ideal to incorporate both structural changes and detail editing into the first rewrite. However, if you can only do one, perhaps because time is short, choose the big-picture option and do the detail in a later phase. If beta readers subsequently criticize the typos you haven't fixed yet, thank them, bolt some temporary ear muffs onto your writerly Viking helmet, and concentrate on the big-picture aspects of their feedback. Check their detail feedback again later to make sure you've dealt with any issues they raised.

Phase 4: Second draft

You've done a major rewrite and it's looking like a book now.

Imagine: All the features of a beautiful valley lie before the author, and more or less in the right order… or so they think. There may be more surface tidiness as well, depending on whether they've had time to do detail corrections yet.

IDEAL FEEDBACK IN PHASE 4	
Professional	Beta reader
Content and structure editor: will focus on the whole-of-book issues of the manuscript and either fix them for you or make suggestions for how you can do so. **Line and/or copy editor**: sometimes the final edit at a word and sentence level will take place now.	Time to engage the team! Big picture issues are still the focus.

Time to engage the team! You will customize your own method of recruiting and managing a beta reader team over the years, book by book.

Some people suggest asking beta readers to go through your manuscript line by line and fix all the errors they see, but that's not what I recommend. Experienced beta readers will often refuse, because they know how long it would take. Those who do say yes are unlikely to have time to give it the attention it deserves. And copy editing is a highly skilled task—few amateurs are really good at it.

Most importantly, however, I believe the best value is to be found in asking your beta readers to give feedback on bigger issues. You are still going to rewrite this manuscript after your beta feedback. So, even if you were planning to ask for a detail edit from your beta readers, now is not the time. Using the valley analogy, you wouldn't wash the windows on all those new houses while earthworks were still going on.

Look for more detail in Chapter 8 about which tasks I do recommend asking of your beta readers.

The size of your team and who you invite will vary due to differences of personality, experience and preference. Remember to try to find several beta readers with different personalities and skill sets to give you different perspectives on your book. Refer back to Chapters 3 and 4 for more detail on the types of beta readers to look for.

 I often have six or eight beta readers on fiction and memoir, but only two or three on non-fiction.

For non-fiction, which I've written and edited for decades, I think carefully about everything my beta readers say, but find it easier to decide how to deal with their suggestions.

Creative writing is more subjective, and I know that I tend to be a people-pleaser. This means there'll be more variety in the opinions and I'm more likely to be swayed by them, even in directions that might not actually be best for my book. Having more beta readers helps insure against that. The extreme opinions tend to cancel each other out, so that I can navigate a more balanced path through the center.

Molly Greene (molly-greene.com), author of the Gen Delacourt Mysteries, prefers a small beta reader team: "I'm now working on my ninth fiction novel, so constructive criticism is old hat for me, and I know what I need from a beta reader. First, I know myself; I'm easily confused and distracted, so I limit the number of opinions and suggestions. Lucky for me, by book #3 or so, I had two fabulous, talented, trusted pre-readers in place who discovered different things in each manuscript and offered their valuable opinions about why certain elements did not work, and sometimes how I might fix them. I send beta readers my third draft. I've done a complete self-analysis and rework of recognizable plot holes and character issues, plus a proof on my Kindle—an excellent way to catch the worst errors. I am not looking for major restructuring at this point in my manuscript—and hopefully, no one will suggest the story needs it! By this point, I am unable to see past the end of my nose and think the book is irredeemable. Sometimes I say so, but most often, since they're also writers, they just get it. This is why I love them. I ask for feedback about obvious errors and what isn't working/doesn't resonate. These boo-boos range from clothing that changes from one color to another, weak intentions on the part of characters, clear mistakes, and you name it."

Interlude: Breathing space

Try to stay away from your manuscript while it's with your beta reader team if you possibly can. When the reports arrive, if they affect you emotionally take time to eat chocolate, seek counseling, cuddle a pet—whatever is your chosen remedy. Some people aren't troubled emotionally by it, but many writers feel resistant to making big changes at this point, especially if they thought they were finished. If you can find the 3H•Heart for it, you may well catapult your book from merely adequate to something quite special. Breathing space helps strengthen you.

Work time: Check/edit/rewrite

Welcome to the apocalypse! It's time to weigh up all that conflicting feedback.

In your imaginary valley, one beta reader will tell you to demolish Village B and put in another river. Another will say you need to make Village B bigger and get rid of all the rivers.

Don't worry, this too is normal. But you are the creator of this little world, and it's your decision.

Your task is to see beyond the suggested solutions to the underlying issues that triggered them. You also need to detect when your beta readers want you to build the valley they see, rather than the one you've seen. It's *your* book. What matches your vision and what doesn't?

> For one novel, my beta readers identified that I'd started the story too early. After a suitable amount of despair, I deleted thousands of words from the front end, and several scenes and characters elsewhere. I sought more beta feedback and discovered the deletions had made it hard for readers to care about my characters or understand their level of danger. I then wrote several completely new early scenes—action instead of backstory. Those scenes were fun to write and ended up being some of my favorites in the book.

> Molly Greene (molly-greene.com) uses only two beta readers and says: "I don't make major changes until both reports are in. At times, feedback about characters or plot elements is contradictory, so I wait, then decide what's right for my book."

A note about staggering your beta readers
Some writers prefer to get all their beta reports at once, while others stagger them, so that one reads the first draft, another the second, and so on.

Chapter 5. When to use beta readers

Halfway through one rewrite, I recruited a new beta reader to test how I'd dealt with issues identified by earlier beta readers. She was initially hesitant because she had a confusing experience when she staggered her beta readers. She said, "Everyone homed in on a different thing and it threw me." It didn't affect me that way—I found it useful. Getting different opinions at different stages might or might not work for you.

The Land of Endless Rewrites

You now enter a cycle of breathing space followed by rewriting—the Land of Endless Rewrites. Some people get stuck in this cycle for years. Others get it out of their hair in a week or two. Find your own path, but try not to keep doing it for the rest of your life. Someone wise once told me: a writer never finishes a book, they just stop.

Phase 5: The final draft

This is it. Congratulations! You've finished. Celebrate!

> **Imagine**: The author surveys a valley that is complete, all its features in place and interacting beautifully. Yes, you can clean those windows now.

IDEAL FEEDBACK IN PHASE 5	
Professional	Beta reader
Copy and/or line editor: edits word by word, line by line, for sense, meaning and correctness. (If you submit to a publisher, there may be further structural editing to come.)	I don't usually recommend a beta reader at this late stage, but sometimes it can be useful to have someone check whether your changes have been effective.

Some writers find it useful to have another beta reader pass through the final manuscript before the editor, to check that the many changes that took place in the rewrite haven't introduced new problems.

A beta reader can also check whether the issues they raised have now been resolved, or whether your chosen solution has actually made it worse. Beware, though, of giving the impression you will automatically do what they suggest, especially at this late stage. As discussed in Chapter 2, you must always be the captain of your manuscript—but especially don't get blown off-course now.

Choice of path — indie publishing or submission to agents?

- If you are **seeking a publisher** but nervous about your writing technique, a quick once-over from a beta reader who is good at grammar and detail might increase your confidence. It can also be a good time to hire a copy editor if you want to make your manuscript as competitive as possible.

- If you **already have a publisher**, it's likely they will ask you for further changes. These may be minor—at a sentence and paragraph level. Or they might ask for something more comprehensive. You might interact with a trusted beta reader while making changes, but the publisher may prefer you avoid anyone else's input at this stage. Communicate with them and be careful to follow their guidance. Experienced publishers will generally be keen to protect your voice and creative vision from outside interference.

- If you are **self-publishing** and can only afford to hire a professional for one phase, this would be the phase to do it. I recommend getting the deepest copy or line edit you can possibly afford.

> This is the point at which I hire a professional editor for my own indie books. Because of the way I manage my beta feedback process, the bulk of the structural editing has already been done in earlier phases, so I generally seek copy editing at this stage. Sometimes, I also seek a professional opinion on specific aspects of the book that I am still undecided about, and this amounts to a light content edit.

Please be aware that, while I use beta readers to empower my own structural editing of my manuscripts, developmental and structural editing are my superpowers—I do them to other people's books for a living. You may find that you get best results when you hire professionals for elements of content and structural editing *as well as* using beta readers in those earlier phases. Find a combination that works for you.

POWER TIP

If you ever do ask your beta readers to make detail corrections, give them a copy of the manuscript in Microsoft Word with Track Changes turned on, which makes all their changes appear in a different color. Beta readers given free rein on your manuscript will make changes you don't like, and even make errors. Guard against it by going through their suggestions one by one.

Typesetting/formatting

This is when your book is laid out ready to be printed, or formatted ready for e-readers, or both.

In a publishing house, print layout will typically be done in specialist software like Adobe InDesign, according to house style, and you'll often have little input into how it looks. Indie publishers sometimes use professional software, outsource it to a professional designer, or use a simpler computer program like Microsoft Word or Vellum to do the layout themselves.

Cover design

Cover design generally also happens at this time. Some publishers will include you in discussions and briefings along the way; others will just show you the cover and give you no opportunity to object or change anything.

If you are self-publishing, you will be overseeing the cover design process, and you can ask your beta readers for feedback about layout, colors, typography, and the blurb. (A good blurb is very hard to write!) You can also use your blog, Facebook groups, or your Facebook page as a forum for testing options.

> For a non-fiction book cover, early reactions had led me to suspect that a design I really liked was causing confusion. I shared it on a Facebook forum for writers, and my suspicions were confirmed. I changed the cover.
>
> For a novel, I blogged about the trend to include human figures on covers and shared two variants: one with a woman in the foreground and one with just a stormy ocean. I set up a poll where people could vote for their preferred cover, and invited people to give their reasons in the blog comments. The post generated an enormous amount of discussion—and confusion! For example, one person said the woman looked scared; another said she looked like she was waiting for a date. One said the sea looked wild; another said it could be a small wave. I had to interpret their comments by looking for underlying fac-

tors. The redesign incorporates elements of each cover, and I believe it's much stronger for the feedback process.

Feedback can be powerful, but it can be confusing, too. Useful outcomes arise from how we manage our response to the comments, not the comments themselves. More on that in Chapter 9.

Phase 6: Proofreading

Proofreading is a whole separate phase from editing. It happens after the book has been laid out, right before it goes to print (print books), or is distributed (ebooks).

The name historically comes from the artwork for printing pages that have been typeset, which are called proofs.

A proofreader checks every letter of every word, every punctuation mark and even every space. They look for consistency in spelling, capitalization, and formatting, and correctness in page numbers, headings, and cross references.

If you are being **traditionally-published**, your publisher will organize proofreading.

Some **self-publishers** use a beta reader in place of a proofreader, but do be aware it's a highly-skilled task that makes a big difference to the professionalism of a book, and it's surprising how many glitches can be missed.

Phase 7: Published!

Celebrate. Your book is out there, being read. And now the reviews start rolling in... more feedback! Always take book reviews with a grain of salt—whether published online or in newspapers and magazines—and yet see what inspiration you can gain for growing your skills in your next book.

POWER TIP

As I work with more and more authors, and write more books myself, I continue to tweak where beta readers slot into the process, my definition of the best people to recruit, and what I ask them to do on each particular project. It's an endless cycle: observe > evaluate > adjust > observe.

A quick recap

- The optimum time to engage a beta reading team is at the second draft, after your rewrite. Because you have already addressed a lot of larger issues, there are less distractions for the reader, so they are able to give you more of the feedback that empowers your book.

- If you choose to engage beta readers at the first draft, be prepared that it might make your task—or theirs—harder.

- Get as much distance as you can from your manuscript between drafts—it helps you to see it with fresh eyes.

- Be careful about beta feedback in the very early stages of your manuscript, especially if you are inexperienced. It can draw you away from your own vision or even make you give up.

Chapter 6. Issuing the initial invitation

In this chapter, we'll look at effective ways to approach potential beta readers. Chapter 7 covers broad principles and practicalities for organizing the people who've said yes. Chapter 8 explores the details of preparing a fruitful briefing document.

In this chapter...

- Attitudes that create an effective beta reading process, and ones that work against us.
- Tips for making the initial request.
- How many to ask.
- Content warnings.

That initial email or approach

The way we word the initial request is often more powerful than we realize. It conveys personality as well as information, and therefore helps us connect with the beta readers we actually want to work with long-term. Be yourself, but also be considerate. A few tips:

- **Spell their name correctly.** (Seems obvious, but this gets overlooked more often than you might think.)
- **Briefly remind them where they know you from.** Make it easy for them.

- If you've met someone personally and kicked around the idea of beta reading, you already have an opening—but **don't assume that offer from three years ago still holds today**, as their situation may have changed.
- **Describe your book *briefly***: working title, genre, word count, which draft it is (e.g. first, second, 37th, final). This could be one short sentence, or a list of dot points. Everyone's busy—make it easy for them to grasp your book concept at a glance.
- **Briefly**—one or two sentences at most—**describe the type of feedback you are hoping for**. (You will give them a more detailed briefing later, when you send the manuscript.) Do you want big-picture feedback about themes and characterization? Do you want a specialist opinion on the technical description in Chapter 22?
- **Offer various formats if you can.** Do they prefer a Word document, a PDF, or an e-reader file? Within your budget and abilities, try to give them what will make the task easiest and most enjoyable for them.
- **Ask in a way that they feel free to say no.** If they feel pressured, they might still say no, but also have a bad taste in their mouth about you for any future interactions.
- **Act like a human.** Add a few honest personal notes of friendship, warmth or humor, if appropriate to the level of connection you have with this person.
- **Mention your schedule.** Be aware that while some beta readers will only spend a couple of hours, others might devote up to twenty hours to the job. You might need to negotiate on timeframes. Don't say you need it tomorrow if that's just your impatience talking. But if you need it

back in time to submit to a contest or a publisher, say so. If your schedule is tight, apologize for it upfront.

How many should I ask?

The number of beta readers you recruit depends on how your brain works and how you are using beta reader feedback.

See "Other ways to recruit beta readers" in Chapter 4 for stories about beta testing teams of up to 100 or more. At the other end of the spectrum, some authors prefer to have only one beta buddy that they work with throughout their career.

Sometimes, the number you prefer on your team varies according to genre—as mentioned in Chapter 5, I use a larger team for the more creative types of books.

As always, no rules. When making your choice, be aware that having too many beta readers can lead to feeling overwhelmed when it's time to process the feedback; too few can mean you lose the balancing effect of hearing different perspectives. Asking a few extra in this initial phase can help cover you if some say no. Develop your own customized process over time, and allow yourself to discover what does and doesn't work for you.

My preference is a team of between three and ten beta readers—some generalists, some specialists, some writers, some non-writers. I engage deeply with their feedback in my self-editing of content and structure, and use it to refine my own vision and purpose for the book.

Chapter 6. Issuing the initial invitation

> David Bruns (davidbruns.com) works with J.R. Olson on a series of military-political thrillers. Their beta team of seven to twelve people includes general readers and specialists. David says: "Selection is key. Every person who is asked to be a beta reader needs to have a reason to be there. We've set up a very structured beta program that has worked well. Briefing them on expectations and putting short questions throughout the book really helped to capture feedback."

My tips for how to manage the feedback process, in this chapter and elsewhere, will focus mostly on this smaller type of team than on the large testing teams of dozens or more.

Attitudes that help

Remember 3H Feedback from Chapter 1?

3H•Humility helps us ask in a way that honors the other person rather than big-noting ourselves. This helps empower the beta reader, who might feel inadequate for the task. If they sense pride from us, they might hold back on criticism that could have been valuable, or some might go to the opposite extreme with harsh feedback designed to take us down a peg or two.

3H•Honesty means that if you're new at this and you don't really know what you want from your beta reader, you can say so. Maybe you can both work it out as you go along—and your openness might be freeing for them.

Attitudes to avoid

I've seen some approaches undermine both the initial answer and the eventual outcome for authors seeking beta readers.

- Don't assume that everyone you approach will want to be a beta reader for you. They might have a hundred reasons for not wanting to do it or not being able to do it.
- Don't assume that you are doing someone a favor by giving them a sneak peek at your book. There is a chance they *will* be delighted, especially if they're already a fan or a friend. But it's safer to assume you are asking for a favor.
- Don't assume they know what a beta reader is, or how to do a beta report. Be ready to give them guidance.

POWER TIP

We often forget that many beta readers are nervous, especially the first time, and worry about hurting our feelings or failing to say anything useful. Some are cool and collected all the way to the core, but in my experience, they are the minority.

If we make beta readers feel relaxed and safe, it helps both of us. Look for ways to make it clear their opinion is valuable, and different to everyone else's opinion. Let them know you'll be getting multiple viewpoints and combining them all—that helps take the pressure off.

Content warnings

Trigger warnings are often controversial among writers, partly because it can be hard to know what's a trigger for someone else. However, when we're recruiting a beta team, it seems only kind and respectful to think about whether a book could potentially cause them trauma. For example, a survivor of domestic abuse or rape might find it hard to read a book covering those themes, and they won't necessarily feel comfortable explaining this to you. Advance warning gives them the opportunity to back out gracefully.

I now think I'd have been wise to warn my beta readers that my murder mystery *Poison Bay* contained a suicide issue.

Some people simply prefer not to read manuscripts containing various levels of violence or explicit sex, so again, it can be helpful to mention the violence or "heat" level upfront.

Similarly, if your book has strong religious or political themes, a reader might be glad to choose whether or not that's the type of thing they want to read.

Beta reading is something people do for pleasure in their spare time, so a part of treating our readers with honor and 3H•Heart is to warn them of things that might make the process unpleasant or even traumatic for them.

Case study: A specialist request that worked for me

When we need specialist input, contacting complete strangers out of the blue can be intimidating for many of us. See if this case study prompts any ideas you'd like to try.

As mentioned previously, I stumbled upon a retired policeman who had published a maritime history book. Social media can be useful for that first tentative contact, but I couldn't find any social profiles for him. However, he had set up a website for his book, and it had a Contact form. This is what I wrote:

> Subject: An unusual request... Police check for a novel??
>
> Message: Hi [name]
>
> I saw your book while searching for a possible NZ police person to fact check my wilderness mystery set in Fiordland National Park.
>
> There is some involvement from the Te Anau police in the plot, and while I interviewed the sergeant in charge there during my research phase several years ago and he gave me masses of excellent tips, there turned out to be questions I didn't ask (a common problem!).
>
> I'm writing to sound you out on whether you may be interested in being a NZ police fact-checker for me. Or if you feel it isn't your cup of tea, is there anyone else you could recommend?
>
> I'm really just looking for someone to tell me: "No, we don't take fingerprints that way," or "We wouldn't talk like that," and you could ask as many questions as you like before you decided whether or not to do it.
>
> I would be open to paying a fee to my "police consultant" (!) but am not a millionaire, so hopefully not a huge fee!
>
> I'm based in Brisbane, and my blog is at smallbluedog.com. (It's my publishing blog, as I work in the publishing industry.) My email is [email address] if you'd like to reply to me.

> I hope your book is doing really well and I look forward to hearing from you.
>
> Belinda Pollard

It disappeared into the ether and I heard nothing for a while. I wasn't even sure if his Contact form was working. However, it turned out he'd been away, and I was elated when he replied and said yes. To make it faster for him, I cut-and-pasted just the police sections into a separate Word document. As mentioned in Chapter 4, the feedback he gave me was stellar. I'm still in awe of just how useful it was.

When making an out-of-the-blue approach to an expert, flag what you want early—even in the subject line, if possible. Try to give a sense of the amount of work that will be required and see what you can do to limit the time commitment for them. Ask for a referral to someone else if they can't help you.

A quick recap

- Don't assume they will want to read for you. Don't act as though you are doing them a favor.
- Honor them, and be honest about what you want, and your own inexperience if relevant.
- Approach them with a reminder about where they know you from, a brief description of your project, the type of feedback you are hoping for, and your schedule.
- Ask in a way that they will feel free to say no if they need to.

Chapter 7. Building a beta feedback relationship

You now have a team of people who've agreed to be your beta readers. I've found that the key to consistently getting useful feedback is to brief your team carefully. Even an inexperienced reader can often give useful feedback if they have been well briefed.

In this chapter, we'll look at broad principles, whereas Chapter 8 goes into detail about the briefing document.

In this chapter...

- Setting the tone.
- Fine-tuning the schedule.
- Formats to offer, and formats to ask for.
- Asking for testimonials.

Begin by setting the tone

I've heard horror stories of people receiving snarky and offensive feedback. Some people can brush it off and keep going; I've encountered others who lose traction or even give up the project altogether.

At the other end of the spectrum, a common complaint in my survey was feedback so fluffy and insubstantial it was a waste of everyone's time.

The best way to minimize the risk of getting either cruelty or fluff is to set the tone upfront.

- Be clear about why you need feedback and **what it will help you achieve**. A brief explanation is usually enough to help a beta reader see that "I loved it" is not going to be sufficient. For example: "I'm learning how to improve my plot, structure and characterization, and your honest feedback on different aspects of my book will help me see the possibilities more clearly."
- Ask them to **mention any strengths they find**, so that you can be sure to retain and develop them in the next draft. Say that honest positive feedback will encourage you and help you persevere through the rewrite.
- Encourage them to **suggest solutions if they wish to**. Some won't be able to think of solutions, which is fine. Some will suggest great solutions. Some will suggest solutions that don't seem quite right to you—but often in the process of realizing what makes that solution a bad fit, you gain a bright idea for a solution that *does* fit.
- If beta feedback seems harsh, often it's because the beta reader thinks of their task as problem-seeking, and **it hasn't occurred to them that their comments might sting**. If you think that might discourage you, adjusting your request can help. For example: "Please be gentle about the negatives if possible, but also be honest with me, as I can't improve it if no one tells me the truth."
- When I need a response faster than usual because of a deadline, I give my beta readers express permission to be brutal in their feedback, because it's faster than being tactful, and **I'd rather have feedback that hurts a little than no feedback at all**. I find my beta readers still tend

to be diplomatic, but at least they are hopefully not wasting time agonizing over their choice of words.

> Jamie was receiving highly critical feedback that seemed to belong in a review rather than a beta report: "I expected that my beta readers would bring the assumption that we're going to make the manuscript work, not that they hate everything about it." That sounds like a good expectation to have, and therefore useful to state in the briefing.

Practical details

I've learned the hard way that it's wise to be as specific as you can about practical details. So many of us tiptoe around, afraid to be pushy, trying not to offend anyone… and then the opposite happens. Everyone ends up confused or frustrated, because no one got what they wanted.

No one likes a bossy author, but we do need to communicate. Ask your beta readers what is most convenient or helpful for them, but also let them know what you want. That crazy one-week deadline might have suited them just fine, if only you'd asked.

Formats to offer your beta readers

Everyone has preferences for how they'd rather read. Within your budget and abilities, try to give them what will make the task easiest and most enjoyable for them. One person I beta read for just automatically sends a Word document, an epub, and a mobi, so I can choose for myself.

- **Microsoft Word document?** If you don't have Word, you can usually create a readable file from Open Office, plus you can compile to Word format from Scrivener.
- **PDF document?** You can create a PDF from Word or Scrivener.
- **A printout?** Some people still prefer this, so if that's what they want, provide it if you can, but don't be afraid to negotiate if printing and postage is too expensive for you.
- I've heard of people setting up a **print-on-demand book** purely so they can provide a paperback to their beta readers. It's not a route I've chosen, but it might even be cheaper than photocopying or printing at home.
- **A format for their e-reader?** This is how I prefer to beta read, and several of my beta readers favor it too.

There are lots of simple ways to convert your manuscript to an ebook. It doesn't have to be beautiful, as it's not the for-sale version.

- Amazon Kindle uses mobi format.
- All other e-readers, including Apple, Kobo and Nook, use epub format.

I write in Scrivener, and use its File > Compile function to very quickly create both epubs and mobis. You can also email a Word document or PDF directly to someone's Kindle, and it will be converted on arrival.

For a small annual fee, BookFunnel (bookfunnel.com) stores ebook files and provides the tech support to help your reader get the file onto their device.

Format for the feedback

When it comes to receiving beta reader feedback, the first thing to consider is: how would **they** like to give their comments? If you possibly can, let them do it the way they find easiest. But again, negotiate if there are problems for you. They might find it just as easy to supply what you prefer.

Some might want to give verbal feedback, either face-to-face or online using something like Skype, but beware that multiple respondents in my survey said they found this less helpful, and sometimes even toxic. Possible problems include:

- During the feedback, you might be trying so hard to look nonchalant (while secretly dying inside) that you can't take in what they're saying.
- Several in my survey reported that all they could remember afterwards were the negatives.
- It can be horribly tempting to start defending yourself.
- Some beta readers also find it confronting to tell you to your face what they didn't like, and they might not realize how stressful that is going to be until they start.
- It can be harder to action verbal feedback. With written feedback, you can look over it and think about it more deeply.

Often the best use of verbal feedback can be in a discussion *after* you've received and pondered the written report. Then you have a chance to draw them out further on what they've said, and seek clarification or possibly nut out solutions together.

These are some of the possibilities for written feedback, which you can suggest if they're not sure:

- A separate text document, written in Microsoft Word or some other word processor.

- In the body of an email.
- Within a Microsoft Word manuscript, using the "Track Changes" feature to insert comments in the margin.
- As notations on an ebook file if you've produced a mobi or epub for them. (There are often difficulties transferring these from one person to another, so do test this method thoroughly before you use it.)
- As written notes on a printout of your manuscript. Don't forget to provide the hard copy, or at least reimburse their printing costs, and pay for return postage. If your beta readers are in other countries this can get incredibly expensive—paper is heavy. They might be able to scan their comments and email or, if the resulting PDF is too large for email, transfer via a service like Dropbox.

Having the discussion now about how to report back to you will help everyone know what to expect, and may just make your job easier if they're happy to provide your preferred format.

Fine-tuning your timeline

Time and again, I have seen two fundamental timeline issues play a crucial role in the ultimate quality of a manuscript:

- Beta readers give the most valuable feedback if they are given the right amount of time—not too much, not too little.
- Writers create their best work if the rewriting timeline allows breathing space. For many people, the creative-brain which makes major changes to a manuscript seems to move more slowly than the typo-correcting correction-brain.

What is the perfect number of days or weeks for these two tasks?

It varies from person to person. However—unless I've got a deadline compressing the schedule—my personal rule of thumb is to try to allow three to six weeks for beta readers to read and make their comments, then a further six weeks for my rewrite after receiving feedback.

This means giving the manuscript to beta readers about twelve weeks before deadline. Does that sound like a long time to you? Or a short time?

We all work differently. If you are working at a different speed and it's producing great results, don't mess with it. However, if you wonder if there's a way to get better results, try experimenting with your timeline.

```
Allowing more time
```
Our society creates a tendency to rush even when speed is not necessary. Weigh these factors:

- Most writers and beta readers are juggling family and community commitments and/or day jobs. They might only be able to spare an hour here or there.

- At average reading speed, it takes six hours or more to read a 90,000 word manuscript. A beta reader must then mentally process their reactions—a task that will require breathing space for the creative-brain. Then they might need more hours to write a report that's both tactful and useful.

- Some people like to read fast and form a quick opinion, but others prefer to immerse themselves in a manuscript and let their mind roam around the possibilities. Neither is better than the other, and your beta reader team might include both types.

The four timeline questions

To prepare your timeline, answer these questions:

1. How long will it take you to get the manuscript ready to send to beta readers? Consider the time you'll need to format and deliver to beta readers as well as the writing and self-editing tasks.

2. How long will your beta readers need? If you're not sure and they're not sure, try to allow a minimum of three weeks if possible.

3. How long will you need to rewrite the manuscript after receiving feedback? If you're not sure, try to allow six weeks if possible. Remember that you might also need to allow time for formatting and other tasks such as writing a synopsis or query letter.

4. What is the submission date for your completed manuscript (to a contest, editor, agent or publisher)?

You might find it useful to print out an empty calendar, such as a template that can be found in Microsoft Word, and jot notes or use highlighters to mark different dates and weeks. Add other major events in your work, health or social life over that time to help you be realistic. If the total time available is less than you'd prefer, choose which phases to adjust.

Try this order:

- If you have a firm submission date, start with Question 4 above and work backwards through the calendar.

- If you don't have a firm submission date, start with Question 1, and from there work forward through the calendar to find your completion date.

When you really are in a hurry
If you need it fast, and your beta readers are busy, modify your request to suit their availability. Perhaps they have time to do a quick read and instinctive response, without going into too much depth.

> For one book I needed a fast turnaround because I had an editor booked and a pre-Christmas release planned. When my schedule slipped, I tried to make it as easy as possible for my busy beta readers to say no if the new timing didn't suit them. I set up a group email so I could send out notifications quickly. All six of these amazing people did in fact meet my insane deadline. Several gave me shorter responses than they normally would due to the time constraints, but between the six we covered all the issues I needed to discuss.

POWER TIP

As discussed previously, two key frustrations that arose from my beta feedback survey were that beta reports were delivered late or not at all, and that beta readers gave a brief response with no useful detail.

A common cause of these two problems (but not the only cause) is time pressure. Consider these possible solutions:

- **Are you failing to provide a deadline** for return? Some people will return it anyway, but for many people, a

Chapter 7. Building a beta feedback relationship

"forever" deadline keeps getting shunted aside in favor of life's little emergencies, to the point where they don't even realize how long has passed. Consider giving them a suggested deadline at the start, and then keep gently in touch with them about how it's going.

- **Are you giving a deadline that is too rushed?** Maybe it suits the speed you work at, but not your beta reader's busy schedule, or even their personality. Maybe they are a person who doesn't know what they think straight away, and needs time to ponder. Could you give them three to six weeks instead?

- **Are you hesitant to ask where the report is?** There are polite, non-pressured ways to ask. Sometimes, an email has gone astray. Sometimes they're embarrassed and keeping a low profile, or feel sure they are too late and you don't need it anymore. Consider asking them—gently—whether they've had any chance to look at it yet, and whether they might still be able to do it.

A quick recap

- Protect yourself from cruel criticism or useless fluff by setting the tone. Outline the type of feedback you need, and ask them to give you positives as well as negatives.
- Check what format they would prefer to receive: ebook, Word document, PDF, printout?
- Ask them to provide their response in your preferred format, but if possible let them supply it in the format that they find easiest.
- Set some type of clear deadline rather than leaving it open-ended, but be reasonable to allow for their busy

lives and the way their minds work. If possible, see if you can allow beta readers three to six weeks.
- If you do have a very tight deadline, be sure to communicate the reasons, and keep them informed if your schedule slips.

Chapter 8. Creating a productive briefing document

I'VE MENTIONED PREVIOUSLY THAT A KEY difference between a useful beta feedback process versus a frustrating one is the briefing, and the heart of this is the briefing document. First, we need to decide, among all the myriad possibilities, what we want to ask our beta readers. Then we need to work out how to ask it in a way that helps them give us what we need. We also need to keep it as short and sweet as possible, so they don't feel overwhelmed.

This chapter contains my discoveries about briefing documents. As always, none of these are rules.

In this chapter...

- Choosing the discussion issues that will be most valuable for your manuscript—big picture versus fine detail.
- Wording your questions in a way that helps your beta readers.
- Organizing questions to help simplify your revision process.

Step 1: Decide your key issues

Big picture versus fine detail

Throughout this book, I've recommended using beta readers primarily to help you with big-picture issues of structure and content, rather than the minutiae of detail editing. I see beta readers primarily as the superheroes of big-picture feedback who empower the developmental phases of our self-editing.

If we were to view a manuscript as a body, big-picture issues would be those that are below the surface, like bones, muscles, blood flow and the nervous system—issues such as the number of characters and their motivation, topics and events that are in or out, and the overall purpose or theme. Detail issues tend to be on the surface, like skin, hair and fingernails—issues such as spelling, grammar, punctuation and sentence construction.

I recommend in all self-editing and feedback processes to start deep and move to surface beautification later in the project. Following are some examples of results from deep, big-picture feedback.

> Janice created a memoir from a series of diary entries, but her beta readers told her they didn't enjoy the format. She says: "I rewrote it in narrative style with just a few diary excerpts, and this time the book was very well received."

> One of my editing clients, Ernest F. Crocker (ernestcrocker.com), had written a fascinating book from a doctor's perspective about people's experiences of medical healing. Together, we worked out that his opening story, though thrilling, was setting up the expectation that it would be a book of miracles. This didn't gel with the rest of the stories, some of which had quite different outcomes. We discovered that by switching the theme to become his person-

al story of discovery—from initially skeptical to a more open position as his medical career progressed—the book became much stronger. It changed the order of the stories and how he talked about them. A publisher acquired the new version, and it's become a bestseller in multiple languages.

I've mentioned my mystery novel, *Poison Bay*, where old friends reunite in a remote New Zealand wilderness. My earliest beta reader asked, "Why did those people agree to go?" I probably would have gone, and hadn't realized lots of others wouldn't. In response to that feedback, I worked through the manuscript, increasing the stakes, enriching backstory, and refining character motivations. A later beta reader challenged me regarding the motivation of one of the villains. She suggested a solution that wasn't quite right for me, and yet it triggered a firestorm in my brain that led to a solution I felt satisfied with.

A member of my public speaking club, critiquing my performance one evening, mentioned that I said "a bit" several times. A light bulb went on over my head. When I got home, I checked for "a bit" in my novel using Scrivener statistics. Sure enough, it was showing up in the dialogue of multiple characters. I did some immediate tweaking. (That Toastmasters member had no idea he was providing beta feedback for a novel!) Consistent, persistent small errors can become a big-picture issue by their very pervasiveness.

Handling detail corrections

There is no doubt that we all do need detail corrections. As an author, I don't tend to use beta readers for this task. For my indie publishing projects, I hire a professional copy editor near the end of the process. For traditional publishing projects, I leave it to the publisher to manage copy editing.

If you do decide to ask beta readers to help you with some detail issues, these are my suggestions:

- Work on the big issues first. Remember the "design your own valley" example in Chapter 5? Don't wash those windows till you've finished the earthworks. And the "body" example in this chapter? Don't shave off leg hairs until the broken bone has been set. Consider having separate beta reading rounds for the two purposes. Start big and wide and deep on the first round, then zoom in to surface details on the later round.

- If you do ask anyone to go through your manuscript in detail on a computer, don't forget to ask them to use Track Changes, the function in Microsoft Word that highlights changes in a different color. The old faithful red pen on paper can be even better, if possible, when detail feedback is coming from a beta reader rather than a professional editor, because you are likely to weigh it up more thoroughly before adding it to your master file. Either way, it's essential that you are able to see everything that has been changed.

- If you do ask a beta reader to make a detail pass through your manuscript, please be aware that you're asking them to do a lot of work. Done properly, a detail pass of a full manuscript is many, many hours of work.

- Don't underestimate the value of having a professional copy editor involved. You will be surprised by the types of issues they pick up that you and your beta readers missed or never even thought of, such as misleading or ineffective sentence constructions, factual errors, inconsistencies, or potential copyright violations. Copy editors are much, much more than just typo correctors.

Checklists versus customized questions

I deliberately avoid prescribing a one-size-fits-all checklist for use with beta readers, especially when the goal is big-picture improvements. I've found that a more organic process of developing customized questions has several advantages:

- It tends to prioritize creativity over conformity.
- It helps sidestep assumptions that there is a right and wrong way to write a book.
- Long lists can sometimes—even accidentally—focus a beta reader's attention on detail instead of big-picture issues.
- The process of choosing areas for discussion, including working out how to word the questions for beta readers, functions as an early phase of developmental self-editing. It forces a writer to analyze their own manuscript as though seeing it through someone else's eyes. As you explain your concerns to your beta readers, you'll be surprised by what becomes clearer in your own mind.

Choose five to seven areas

I recommend developing a list of five to seven main issues you wish to ask your beta readers about, and using those issues to create your questions.

Limiting the number of discussion areas helps in several ways:

- It helps avoid a feeling of overwhelm for both reader and writer. Multiple pages of questions can seem intimidating, and *look* like they're going to be hard to answer even if they aren't.

- Limiting the scope makes it more likely you'll get deeper, higher-quality feedback on the issues that really will make a difference to the development of your book. Beta readers can spend more of their available time on each question.
- Asking your questions in five to seven sets will make it easier for you to process the feedback later. You will be able to more naturally organize the responses into sets, and compare the responses of different beta readers.

If you are a visual thinker or big-picture person, a whiteboard or large piece of art paper can be a good way to work on your list of issues. Try drawing a mindmap where ideas radiate out from a central purpose, or use the concept of spokes from a wheel. Alternatively, just clump related ideas together in different parts of the space. Each clump or spoke might become one of your five to seven areas, or one clump might produce multiple areas.

If you are detail-focused and find that you are producing lists that are just too long, do a brain dump and write all those ideas down to unclog the stream. You might write it by hand, but if you do prefer to do it on a computer, I suggest printing out your lists for the next phase—it activates different parts of the brain when we work by hand. Go through with a pen or pencil, marking the ones that leap out at you as most important. Lay the pages side-by-side on a table and look for connections between the marked issues. Consider using different symbols or different highlighter colors as you discover issues that seem to belong together in similar categories. Each category might become one of your five to seven main issues.

Once you've been through this process with one book, you will find that in the next book, questions for your beta readers are emerging even while you are still in the first draft or early edits. Jot them down so they're easy to remember when it's time for beta readers, for example in a dedicated notebook or by creating a dedicated research folder in a Scrivener project. By the time you're briefing your beta team, you might find that you have unconsciously resolved some of your questions—another excellent side-effect of thinking about it as you go. You might be able to tweak other questions to become even more useful.

Thought starters

Some writers can readily decide what their five to seven areas are going to be. Others find it more difficult, and that's fine. If that's you, try using the following ideas to trigger more thoughts:

- What sections of your manuscript are you least confident about?
- What writing techniques do you struggle with?
- There might have been a difficult decision you had to make about what to include or exclude, or where to take the story. Beta feedback is your opportunity to check whether or not you have found an effective solution.
- Did you write with a clear purpose in mind? For example, a memoir about domestic violence might be written to encourage others going through the same thing. A non-fiction book might seek to teach a particular skill. A novel might aim, through story, to challenge people to protect the environment. Whatever your underlying purpose, seek feedback on whether or not you've achieved it.

It can also be helpful to ask your beta readers which writers or books your manuscript reminds them of. This information is useful in marketing, choosing bookstore categories, or when querying literary agents.

Genre-specific prompts

Following are some broad areas to consider for different basic genres. Don't feel you must cover all these areas—just use them as thought triggers.

- Fiction: characters, setting, plot, structure, dialogue, description, point of view, first or third person, past or present tense, fast or slow pace. There will also be common issues in each sub-genre—for example, effective world-building for fantasy or subtle clue-dropping for crime.

- Memoir: everything that applies to fiction, plus whether you've revealed too much or too little of yourself, and issues related to how it might affect your relationships with real people you've mentioned.

- Non-fiction: structure, purpose, clarity, length, uniqueness.

Using a SWOT Analysis to refine your list

Sometimes, a SWOT Analysis (Strengths, Weaknesses, Opportunities, Threats) can help refine a list of areas to discuss with beta readers. When a SWOT Analysis is used for business, strengths and weaknesses are typically internal, while opportunities and threats are external.

- Internal issues could be characteristics of yourself as a writer or within your manuscript.

- External issues might include deadline constraints or market forces affecting publishers or the book-buying public.

However, if you don't find those categories useful, feel free to use it in whatever way means the most to you. This is not about "doing it right," but about finding a tool that helps. Draw a simple table with two columns and two rows.

Strengths	Weaknesses
What is good about your manuscript and your writing technique? Write brief notes in this square. (This can be expanded after you've received feedback.)	What areas do you know you struggle with? Jot them down in this square. (You might add some extras after you've heard back from your beta readers.)
Opportunities	**Threats**
Examples: What might you be able to achieve with this book? How will it enhance your writing career or complement whatever other careers you have? What are the marketing and collaboration possibilities for the book?	Examples: Are other writers in a better position to write such a book? If timing matters, might someone else finish and publish first? Is the market overcrowded with this type of book?

POWER TIP

If you used the SWOT Analysis and found it helpful, go back to it once you've received your beta feedback.

Add to your notes in each square. Enhance the positives in line with their comments (avoid false modesty if you can), and refine the negatives to add things you hadn't thought of, or to add subtlety to the descriptions.

This SWOT Analysis can be even more interesting to pull out again in the future when working on further books. It helps track growth.

Step 2: Develop your questions

Use your five to seven issues to develop five to seven questions (or groups of questions). How you word your questions influences the value of the feedback you receive.

The value of cluster-questions

It can be useful to ask several questions in one clump which expand in multiple directions on a particular theme. Each beta reader's mind will lock onto elements of the grouping that mean something to them. It's fine for each beta reader to focus on different things.

Avoid jargon, mostly

I recommend avoiding jargon most of the time, because:

1. Your beta reader might not understand it, if they haven't read the blogs or been to the workshops. They might feel confused or alienated. They might give answers that you find confusing—because they're responding to what they thought you meant.

2. If they do understand the jargon, their thoughts might immediately start running on rails like a train, instead of generating unique creative insights.

```
Wide-open questions versus closed,
controlling questions
```

We'll take a short excursion into the psychology of communication here—but feel free to skip this part if it's not of interest to you.

The most effective questions tease out a beta reader's raw reactions to a manuscript *instead of inviting a judgment*. Wide-open questions tend to elicit instinctive, creative reactions instead of controlled, right-versus-wrong reactions.

Wide-open questions increase the possibility of unexpected answers. Unexpected answers might initially feel chaotic, but they can trigger sparks of brilliance as your mind explores them.

Let's work through an example. In creative writing you might worry whether you are telling the reader too much about what people are thinking, instead of just letting it emerge naturally. This is sometimes referred to using the writer-jargon "show, don't tell."

- ✘ Train-track question: "Did I show enough, or was there too much telling?"
  The jargon might be confusing, and the question invites your beta readers to make a judgment they might not be comfortable to make. Some readers might rush to reassure you the book is fine (even if you really are over-telling) and others might assume there's a problem and start seeing it everywhere.

- ✔ Wide-open cluster-question: "Did you feel like you could see and hear and feel the events as they unfolded? Were there any places where you'd have liked to know more? Any places where I gave too much information?"
  This type of question gives you less control over the

responses, but increases the likelihood of insightful reactions.

If after receiving feedback you still wanted more clarity about the specific "show, don't tell" question, you could ask a follow-up question, stating the particular concern. By asking it as a follow-up instead of in the initial set of five to seven, you would avoid coloring the first, instinctive responses.

When to use yes/no questions

As a journalism student, I was taught not to ask "closed questions"—questions that invite a very brief answer, often just yes or no. However, because a beta reader gets all the questions at once—unlike a news interview where a person usually answers one question at a time—I do find that closed questions can get a topic started if they are mixed with open questions in a cluster-question.

Here's an example. Instead of asking: "Did I have too many characters?" you might ask: "Did you like and engage with the characters? How easy was it to get to know them and keep track of them all?"

Here's another example.

- ✘ Closed question: "Was the book too short?"
  This asks the beta reader to make a value judgment, and hints that someone already thinks it's too short, potentially coloring their answer.

- ✔ Combination cluster-question: "Did you like the length of the book? If so, what did you like about it? Were there places you'd have liked to know more, or less?"

There will always be times, however, where the type of relationship you have with a beta reader makes it quite appropriate to declare your focus upfront. You might write a cluster-question like this: "I've been concerned it might be too short. What do you think? Do you think readers will like it this length? Or did you notice any parts where you'd have liked to know more?" This invites them to think beyond their personal preference, and also to do some troubleshooting if they'd like to.

Three useful questions I ask every time

These three questions have been so powerful for me that I now add them to every beta reader briefing document:

1. **"What did you like about it?"** As discussed previously, beta readers often think of their job as "looking for problems" which can sometimes accidentally tilt their opinions and also lead to discouragement for you. Their positive comments will help you develop a useful understanding of your strengths, lift your spirits in the hard work that lies ahead, and help you avoid accidentally getting rid of things that readers actually liked.

2. **"Anything else?"** I add this question at the end, after my other customized questions. Beta readers will talk about issues that never occurred to me. I've had absolute gold emerge from these answers.

3. **"Would you be willing to write a testimonial that I can use in marketing?"** But I try to make it easy for them to say no if they'd prefer not to write a testimonial.

POWER TIP

If you intend to self-publish, snippets of testimonials can be used as "puff quotes" in marketing your book. If you are seeking traditional publication, you might be able to use them on your website or even perhaps in query letters. These snippets are genuine reader responses, which are valued in today's world.

> The testimonial comments I've received from beta readers for my indie projects have generally appeared in full on the first page inside the cover, and in a shorter form in other marketing materials.

Step 3: Create your briefing document

Everyone will have their preferred way of briefing their beta feedback team. I create a Word document and email it to each beta reader with a personal message in the email. My priorities for this Word document are to:

- Provide enough background to help my beta readers give useful responses, without overwhelming them with too much extra reading.
- Make it as simple as possible for them to answer, so it doesn't waste their time.
- Make it as straightforward as possible for me to process the responses. The questions have the effect of pre-organizing their responses according to theme.

The introductory information

What you say in your summary at the head of the briefing document can set the tone and help avoid the "useless fluff" versus "dispiriting criticism" extremes of beta feedback.

These are some of the types of information I include in the introduction:

- A brief outline of the purpose of the book.
- A description of the manuscript's current state, and what I **don't** expect my beta readers to do about it. For example, I might say: "There are still a lot of typos, but please ignore them for now."
- The freedom to answer as many or as few of the questions as they want.
- A clear deadline, stating a second fallback deadline so they know the outer boundaries, and a clear reason as to why I need it at that time—for example, a launch date or deadline with my editor.

Adding the list of questions

Below the introduction, I insert my five to seven issues into a one-column table, with an empty row below each question where beta readers can type their answer.

The sample document pictured here—an actual briefing document I used for one project—is available as a free download at usefulwritingtips.com if you'd like to "reverse engineer" it to get further ideas for your own briefing documents.

In this example, two of my six beta readers typed their responses into the Word document I sent. The rest wrote their responses in a separate format, but followed the general list of my questions. Some answered all the questions; some only a few. I was pleased they felt free to take their own approach to it, and I regard it as a successful beta feedback experience.

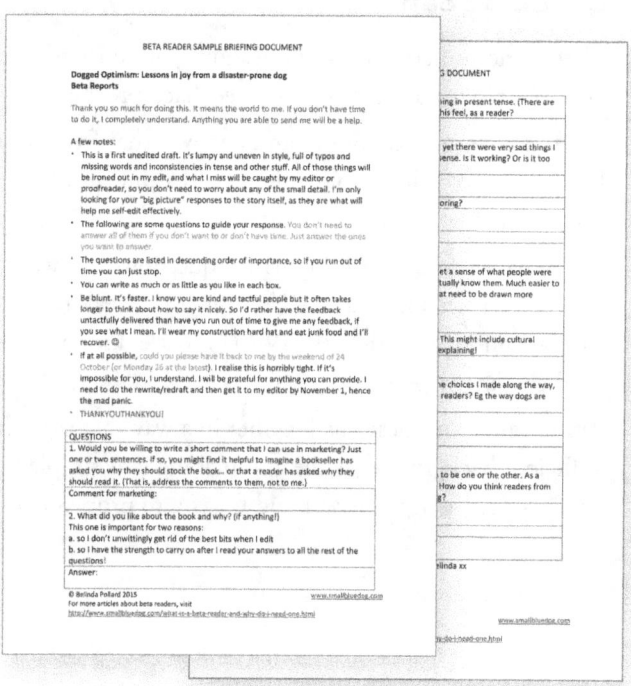

The sample briefing document pictured above is available as a free download at usefulwritingtips.com.

POWER TIP

I continue to refine the way I ask questions. I am always tweaking my beta feedback process. In the business world they call this "continuous improvement" and I believe it's a valuable concept for us as authors, too—not only in how we continually improve our writing, but also in how we improve our feedback and publishing "procedures."

Chapter 8. Creating a productive briefing document 111

A quick recap

- There is no prescribed list of questions you must ask, nor any "right" way of managing the feedback process.
- Try to ask your questions in an open way that frees your beta readers to tell you what they really think and to provide their own perspective.
- If you have trouble deciding which questions you want to ask, try assessing your book's Strengths, Weaknesses, Opportunities and Threats (SWOT) to see if it gives you further clarity.
- Try to put your questions together in a way that provides sufficient background, while also making it as simple as possible for them to answer and for you to process later.

PART 3:
What to do with the feedback you receive

How to protect your vision for your book and make the most of your beta feedback, even when it's confusing or contradictory.

Chapter 9. How to apply the feedback you receive

First, there will be chocolate, weeping and despair. But after that?

How you respond to feedback is a key element of the success of your beta reader management.

But don't worry if you don't have it all figured out immediately. Give yourself permission to grow in this ability over the course of your writing career.

In this chapter...

- Different instinctive reactions to beta feedback, and attitudes that can help.
- The importance of time and space.
- Several techniques for weighing the results.

How people react to beta feedback

Reactions vary from author to author, but it's not uncommon to be devastated by your beta feedback. I've noticed criticism tends to hurt more if the author is just starting out, or the manuscript is strongly connected to a relationship or their self-image in some way. It may also be that it hurts more for people-pleasers, but that one would be hard to measure.

The important thing to remember is that if you do experience some negative emotions at first sight

of beta reports, it doesn't mean the beta reader process has failed, or they weren't good beta readers, or you're not a good writer.

> Kylie says: "I gave a copy to my best friend, and I could tell she didn't love it. Because her opinion was so important to me, this crushed my spirit. It took some inner pep talks and self-soothing to bounce back." (But Kylie did bounce back.)

> Zachary says: "I got good, honest feedback that hurt my feelings and pride at the time, but ultimately it was excellent advice that helped make my writing better."

> Mystery author Molly Greene (molly-greene.com) says: "I have never felt devastated over a beta report. Overwhelmed with the editing task ahead? Absolutely. Annoyed when I'm shown what I missed and what I need to repair? You betcha. So I take a break from the manuscript, to clear my mind and prepare for the task ahead."

Whatever your reaction looks like, Molly has a great tip there about the value of "distance"—the breathing space we mentioned in Chapter 5.

It's normal to feel psychological pressure of some kind in response to criticism of your manuscript. You will move past it, just as countless other writers have done.

And you will become a stronger writer every time you do it. It develops writerly muscle—like resistance training at the literary gym.

Despite your best efforts to brief them for consistent results, your beta reader team will have sent in reports that look very different, and are organized in different ways. They might say completely contradictory things about your book—sometimes even within the one beta report.

This, too, is normal, and not a sign that the process isn't working.

Managing all these responses can feel like you're herding cats (or, some days, panthers), but when you dive in and do it with enthusiasm it makes for an amazing beta feedback process.

Helpful attitudes

These are some ways 3H Feedback (outlined in Chapter 1) can apply to the response process.

3H•Humility helps us to listen carefully and be open even to feedback we disagree with.

3H•Honesty after reflection sometimes helps us to see that they were right, or even if their suggestions are not quite right for our book they might trigger other ideas that *are* right.

3H•Heart gives us the courage to do this thing—to love our manuscript enough that we'll do what's best for it rather than just cling to its original form or give up altogether.

3H•Heart helps us stand back from the feedback and connect with our true purpose in writing, so that we can weigh up the suggestions we've received.

3H•Heart is also about doing the rewrites, even when we thought we were finished—because our book is worth it and the bigger picture of our writing career is worth it.

Should you defend your manuscript?

There is no need to argue with your beta reader about a piece of feedback you disagree with. It tends not to lead anywhere useful.

Just think carefully about it with an open mind and a dollop of 3H•Humility, then make your own choice. It's ultimately your decision whether or not to adopt their suggestions.

There can, however, be value sometimes in asking for more information or clarification. Some won't have time to think about your book any further, but others will have said in their response to feel free to ask questions.

Some beta readers might challenge you later about why you didn't follow their advice, although I have never had this happen. Perhaps just say that you appreciated their input very much, but after careful thought you decided to take a different course.

Don't rush

Before we get into the details of your response, may I first say this:

> **The less experienced you are as an author, the more important it is not to rush your response to beta feedback.**

Eager New Author receives a beta report that says the zombies in Chapter 3 are all wrong and have to go. Eager New Author rushes off and removes the zombies. Next day Eager

New Author receives another beta report saying the zombies are a masterstroke, and need to be developed further to make this the best book in history.

Sometimes, we rush in for emotional reasons: we want to release the psychological pressure and feel better about the book. Time and space, however, are powerful tools.

> Nina says: "I changed the first chapter based on a beta reader's idea. The second beta reader hated that new version, so I changed it again. I ended up rewriting the first chapter eight times, and I now think my original version would have been fine."

> Debra says: "I got some great advice but overall I probably took on too much of it and should have stuck to my vision more."

If you have the courage to sit with the psychological pressure a little longer—or disperse it with a favored stress reliever such as exercise—instead of immediately attacking the manuscript, you will get a much more solid result from beta feedback. My suggested process:

1. Read all the feedback. If possible, wait for every report to come in before beginning your response.

2. Give yourself as much distance as possible. Time is the best form of distance, if you have the luxury. I also recommend getting away to do other things—go to a movie, or out for coffee, or for a walk with the dog. At the very least, wait overnight. The brain is

busy while we sleep; take advantage of sleep's power if you can. I find that when I reread beta feedback the next day, the items that made me either despairing or even angry yesterday now read quite differently. I find myself thinking: "Oh, is that what they said? Why was I so worried about it?" I can see beyond the internal noise of my initial knee-jerk reaction to the useful gems contained in the feedback.

3. Now, read it all again. What ideas are coming through now? Can you see how Reader A and Reader B actually have some things in common, even though yesterday they seemed to be polar opposites? These are things that take time to develop in the back cupboards of our brains.

Trust yourself

Alert: if a piece of advice just doesn't feel right to you no matter which way you look at it, listen to your instinct.

You don't want to just ignore the advice—consider it carefully and respectfully.

But don't ignore your instincts about your own book; balance is essential. 3H•Humility is good, but loss of your story is bad. Remember that 3H•Heart gives you the courage to make changes if appropriate, but also to protect your vision and purpose when necessary.

Look for patterns

Look for patterns in your beta reports. Are there things that everyone says? Are there complete opposites among the reactions?

Chapter 9. How to apply the feedback you receive

If there are opposites, is there a common feature to what they've said that isn't immediately obvious?

Weigh the results

Not all beta readers are created equal—and it doesn't necessarily depend on their experience in publishing or how many books they've written themselves. Some are just better at detecting the strengths and weaknesses of your particular manuscript, and the possible ways you can change it.

Also learn to look beyond the comment to what's underneath. Perhaps you can re-purpose the advice. For example, you might reject the advice: "never use an adverb." However, it might be pointing out something you do need to know: that you have used too many adverbs, and used them in ineffective ways so that they stick out. You can go on a "search and destroy" for only the adverbs that weaken a sentence.

> Beth says: "I've received incredible feedback from beta readers, and even if I don't actually use their suggestion it always illuminates something new for me that I hadn't thought about before. Based on feedback, I've made huge structural changes in manuscripts that made the story so much better."

The following are several techniques you can try. Don't feel forced into using any of them, but on the other hand perhaps be open to trying one that doesn't at first sound like you. You might try it and find that, with a tweak or two, it becomes your favored method.

You might end up using different methods for different genres, and even for different books within the same genre. Your technique for evaluating the reports will continue to grow, and you will also face new challenges as you go along.

1. The spreadsheet

This one suits analytical thinkers, but even if you're more intuitive, give it a try and see if it helps.

- Make a spreadsheet collating all the responses to a particular question.

- You might want to spreadsheet all the questions, or only the most contentious questions, or only the ones you find the hardest to resolve in your mind.

- Look for both agreement and contradiction. Compare it against the experiences and personalities of each beta reader.

- What might have influenced the answer they gave, and how is it likely to apply to your target readership?

- If useful, try scoring the different responses, weighted according to each beta reader's background, their similarity to or ability to understand your target reader, and how well they get you and your book.

- While you're at it, what can you learn for next time about the usefulness of the questions you asked and how you will manage the beta feedback process?

2. Pros and cons

If you have one really controversial issue, like the dead-or-alive ending of my book *Dogged Optimism* which I'll work through in the case study which follows, you might find it useful to do a list of pros and cons for that one issue.

- Rule up a sheet of paper, a whiteboard, or a Microsoft Word document with two columns: mark one "For" and the other "Against," or whatever headings work best with the particular issue you're trying to resolve. For example, for *Dogged Optimism* I could have headed them "Dead" and "Alive."
- How your brain works will influence whether you'd rather do it onscreen or by writing manually—maybe try both!
- A whiteboard is useful for some. There's something about big elbow movements that activates the brains of kinesthetic learners (people who learn through movement).
- Enter a summary comment from each beta reader below the appropriate heading. See if you can condense it to just a few words, as that will make it easier for you to gain a quick grasp of the issues once they are all placed on the page, screen, or board. While choosing those summary words, your mind is also working on developing your manuscript.
- Don't forget your own opinion. Enter your own thoughts for and against that particular issue.
- If you find it useful, give a rating from 1–10 to each comment, to help you add up the cumulative value of the various thoughts.

3. Color and movement

This one can be good for the visual and kinesthetic (movement oriented) thinkers.

- Print out all the feedback—yes, on actual paper! The texture and movement of rearranging the pieces is part of the technique.

- Get yourself a set of highlighters in various colors. I have a set of eight, and they are all different colors. (Hands up, who else likes stationery?)
- On a separate sheet, create a key that shows what each color means. For example, character issues might be blue, yellow for setting, pink for dialogue, orange for theme. I've discovered that it's best not to expect yourself to remember the meaning of each color.
- Go through each report and highlight different kinds of issues by color.
- Create a list or mind map of the connections created.
- This is another technique where a whiteboard might help you access a different part of your brain.

4. Instinct

This one can be good for intuitive people.

- Read all the reports, quietly and carefully.
- Put them away and let it all marinate.
- Then come back to a clean sheet of paper, your whiteboard or a computer program like Scapple, and make a list or a mind map of all the points that have stayed with you.
- Be aware that a drawing pad might be better for you than lined paper. Lined paper sometimes feels restrictive.

Fans of a particular writing technique

Some beta readers will be fans of a particular school of writing and will note every place you have diverged from it.

I always enjoy having various suggestions from my beta readers, but thankfully mine tend to offer their discoveries in a less intense way. If it's an idea I haven't heard of before, I go online and do a little research. Then I make my own decision.

If you are finding one set of feedback particularly strident or disruptive, try these tips:

- **Be free.** You don't have to agree. Your vision, your book.
- **Be gracious.** They thought it was part of their task, and they are trying to help you. You don't need to get into a debate (unless you have the type of relationship where both of you might enjoy that).
- **Be creative.** There might be some aspect of the feedback that helps you, if you adapt it.

Case study: Making difficult choices

For the light memoir *Dogged Optimism*, I had written the ending when my terrier, Killarney, was fourteen years old and pleasantly dotty. It had always been my goal *not* to write one of those "humorous" books where the dog dies in the end, because I find such books depressing, even though they can be very popular.

However, when the publication date loomed—three years after I'd written the ending—Killarney had indeed left this world at the grand old age of nearly seventeen. Each of my beta readers knew me well enough to know she had died.

When their reports came in, several of my beta readers were puzzled and disappointed that I hadn't gone right to the end of the dog's life. I could tell that the omission had affected them, which meant it could potentially disappoint some of my target readers.

So I began to wrestle with whether I needed to add another three years of stories to the end of my manuscript. It would destroy my publishing schedule, but if that had to happen, it had to happen.

More importantly, it would change the arc of the story to become a different book with different themes and a different resolution.

I argued with myself about it, talked to several trusted people, did some weeping and some praying. I hid for a few days, slept badly, and became a bit of a grouch (yes, all part of the wonder of feedback processing when it's a big issue).

Then I rolled up my sleeves and scrutinized the outline. What stories would I add? This was a light memoir needing an upbeat ending—it couldn't suddenly end in misery. What would be the upward trajectory that the death of Killarney took me on? Perhaps it would be something about my puppy, Rufus, acquired a couple of months after I wrote that initial ending.

For two years I had two dogs. Perhaps I could tell their merging stories, then continue on past Killarney's death to show how Rufus had brought my story onto an upswing again?

But there were so many stories to tell about Rufus, and they were utterly different. Killarney was a bossy terrier with Small Dog Syndrome who viewed the human race as her public; Rufus was a herding breed—super-intelligent, athletic, and devoted to his tiny circle of trusted humans.

Killarney's behavioral problems and my mismanagement of them was the organizing principle of the plot and humor in the existing manuscript. Rufus's behavioral problems and my mismanagement of them had a completely different flavor.

As I wrestled with all these issues, trying to do my best for my book and my readers, clarity emerged: what I had was two books. The second book would focus on Rufus, but begin with his life's overlap with Killarney, and her final decline.

My confidence in the original ending returned, but not just because I like happy endings. It was the *right* ending. It showed the growth—mine and hers—and ended on the right arc.

I dived in to a thorough rewrite, making both small and large changes to bring that movement into clearer focus. And then I spent a surprising amount of time crafting a one-page afterword which explained that Killarney had left, but I had the company of Rufus as my "red healer."

I didn't know whether readers would approve my decision, but I now felt calm and settled. Later, I was encouraged by statements like these in reviews:

- "The book is fun, easy to read, and heart-warming. And it does NOT end with the death of her beloved dog."

- "Plot spoiler alert: it was a good decision to end the book before Killarney dies, so that the tone remains upbeat and optimistic—and it's good news too that just when Killarney is entering old age, [Belinda] acquires another dog, and so the premise for a sequel to this book, which I look forward to reading."

- "*Dogged Optimism* is an accomplished, inspiring piece of writing that had me completely hooked from the first page to the unexpected and gratifying end."

For those reviewers at least, I did the right thing. And more importantly, I refined, strengthened and trusted my vision for my book.

Sometimes, we'll confront issues with our manuscripts that have no easy answers. We can't expect our beta readers to make the big decisions for us. We have to find our own path to the best decisions we can make using the skill and knowledge we have at this point.

The action plan

It's now time to commence your rewrite. How do you keep track of all those tips you've learned about your manuscript?

- Organize your thoughts and reactions in a way that makes sense to you: by manuscript location, by theme, by type of problem.
- Some people find it useful to develop a checklist of required changes and work through them one by one.
- Some like to stick with a mind map, and follow one branch of the mind map at a time.
- Some like to write all the important thoughts on a whiteboard or on sticky notes on the wall, and erase or remove them one by one as they're dealt with.

There might be one big issue you need to consider as you go through the whole manuscript.

Let's say for example that you're writing a memoir. The big question that has emerged as an organizing theme for the whole book might be "how did it change you?" This one question holds the whole book together, and helps you decide whether to include or delete certain events, scenes and characters. Use reminders that work for you:

- Write it in large letters on a piece of paper, and stick it to the wall near your desk or even to the side of your computer screen (I have a surprising number of things stuck to the edges of my computer screen).
- Set yourself a reminder on your phone or computer that pops up each day.

- If you are in an intensive rewriting weekend, for example, you might even set a reminder every hour.

We forget high level issues so easily once we get engrossed in the rewrite. Each reminder helps bring us back to what we have decided to do.

Self-editing tips

The full task of self-editing is a topic for another book, but here is my basic process. When doing the big rewrite after beta reader reports, I recommend a wide-narrow-wide approach. Imagine you're standing on the mountaintop of Chapter 5 holding a camera with a big expensive zoom lens, surveying the landscape of your manuscript. Start with a wide angle, zoom in steadily to a narrow view, and then pull back out to wide again.

Fix the big stuff before the little stuff, because a lot of the little stuff gets deleted or changed as the big stuff moves around. There would be no point polishing the banister in one of those houses in your valley, only to have the house itself be demolished, renovated, or moved to Village B.

This is how it might work:

Step 1. Wide angle
Start with big issues. These are just a few examples to get you thinking, not an exhaustive list:

- **Fiction**: Number of characters, first or third person voice, overall movement of the plot, whether the theme or metanarrative develops well throughout, other large issues.
- **Memoir**: Clarity of theme or purpose, number of characters and how deep they go, your rationale for including or excluding events, other large issues.

- **Non-fiction**: Clarity of theme, effectiveness of structure, whether the argument builds as the book develops, whether some material needs to be added, or some removed.

Step 2. Zoom in

Work on fine detail: typos, grammar, excessive adverbs, clunky dialogue tags, too much capitalization, inappropriate use of jargon, consistency and correctness of spelling for names and words that have variant spellings, sentence flow and meaning.

Step 3. Wide angle again

Resolve any new problems you created in Step 1 or Step 2. Some examples:

- **Fiction**: you changed the weapon to a dagger in Chapter 37 but foreshadowed bow and arrow in Chapter 10.
- **Memoir**: your amusing scene with Aunt Beatrice in Chapter 3 now needs to be deleted because she no longer appears in the rest of the book.
- **Non-fiction**: you rearranged chapters so that the how-to in Chapter 16 now comes before the explanation of why the reader needs to do it in Chapter 18.

Some writers might choose to go through the whole manuscript doing all the big-picture edits, then do a completely new round for the detail, followed by a third round for newly-created or persistent issues. Others will do it a chapter at a time: wide, narrow, wide. Try different combinations and see what works for you.

Thanking your beta readers

I like to send my beta readers a quick thank you message as soon as possible after I've received their report. Keep in mind that while some beta readers will be relaxed about their role and have already moved on to 27 other tasks, others will be waiting anxiously, worried about whether they've given us what we were hoping for.

Because of my thinking processes and schedule, it might be a week or two before I think deeply about or act upon all their feedback, so I often keep the door ajar in this first message by asking if I can come back to them later if I have any questions.

There are various other ways to thank beta readers. Some people like to give a thank you gift—a book voucher, chocolates, a book bag, a mug, something they've made. Some give a copy of the finished book in either ebook or paperback formats. Some even have a party for their beta readers.

> I like to thank my beta readers publicly at the start of my books. These are some of my general policies (but you will of course establish your own):

- I mention their work if appropriate and relevant.
- For those who are authors, I give credit to their books or writing career.
- For specialist beta readers, I give more detail about what they did, and sometimes a mention for a relevant charity.

I always ponder about which order to list them and vary it to suit.

A quick recap

- It's normal to feel some type of stress or psychological pressure when you receive your beta reports. It's not a sign that the process isn't working.

- The less experienced you are as an author, the more important it is not to rush your response to beta feedback.

- Look for patterns in the feedback, weigh the results, and trust yourself and your purposes for your own book.

- A spreadsheet, a table of pros and cons, printouts marked with different colored highlighters, and mind maps can all help untangle confusing feedback. The method that works best for you may depend on your personality and experience.

- Once you have evaluated the feedback, create an action plan for your rewrite.

- When you begin self-editing, it can be helpful to make big-picture changes, then correct detail, then do another pass to see if any problems have been introduced at the big-picture level.

- Look for ways to honor your beta readers by thanking them, including in the acknowledgments section of your book.

Where to now?

Thank you for traveling through this book with me. I hope it encourages you to continue growing your skills and writing your best book.

Beta readers are the quiet superheroes of today's publishing. Authors like you who persevere and grow through the feedback process are champions too. And you become a superhero when you do this task for someone else's manuscript. (Cape and tights optional.)

Please keep helping other writers. The benefits flow both ways. I have found that the more beta reading I do for friends, the more I grow and learn. My methods and techniques as both a beta reader and a writer continue to evolve.

I'd love to see you at my blog, on social media or at one of my in-person or online workshops.

Please visit **usefulwritingtips.com** to:

- **Download your free copy of the Seven Phases of Feedback flowchart (Chapter 5).**
- **Download a free sample briefing document (Chapter 8).**
- **Get information, resources and an expanding list of useful books to help you continue growing as a writer.**

I wish you ever-increasing success as you manage the feedback process on your manuscripts, and grow into the writer you were born to be.

If you enjoyed this book and found it useful, I'd love it if you left an honest review on Goodreads, social media, your blog or any of the online bookstores, and told your writing friends about it. It helps me more than you know. Thanks for spending this time "talking writing" with me!

Belinda Pollard

Glossary

3H Feedback: Humility, Honesty and Heart. Humility honors the other person. Honesty tells the truth but also includes looking for the good as well as the bad. Heart includes both courage and compassion.

alpha reader: sometimes used to differentiate various phases of feedback. Not a definition used in this book.

beta reader: in this book, anyone who gives feedback on a draft or "beta" version of a manuscript, for free, is referred to as a beta reader. (In this book, paid professionals are referred to by other titles.)

copy editor: in this book, a copy editor is a paid professional who edits line by line immediately prior to typesetting for such issues as sense, flow, grammar, spelling and punctuation.

demographics: personal characteristics such as age, sex, education level, nationality, religion etc.

developmental editor: in this book, a developmental editor is a paid professional who works on a manuscript in the developmental stages, giving suggestions regarding deep issues such as content, structure and purpose of the book.

fiction: a product of the imagination; non-factual; not a true story; a novel in one of many genres, such as romance, mystery, young adult.

genre: style, category or type of book. Can refer to broad types such as factual versus fictional, or sub-types such as mystery versus romance. Usually pronounced _zhon-ra_ or _djon-ra_.

indie author: in this book, someone who self-publishes to a professional standard.

memoir: a form of creative non-fiction based on the author's memories.

non-fiction: writing that is based on fact. Includes a wide range of topics such as how-to, self-help, textbooks, biography, history, information.

proofreader: in this book, a proofreader is a paid professional who makes the final pre-publication check of "page proofs" correcting such issues as grammar, spelling, punctuation, consistency and layout.

royalty: a percentage of book sales paid to the author/s.

self-publishing: the author manages the complete process of publishing and distribution. Some will do all the work themselves; some will hire professionals for various tasks or phases.

traditional publishing: the publisher manages editors, cover designers, distribution and various other phases of publishing. They then pay the author a royalty. In traditional publishing, the author should not have to pay to participate.

Index

Symbols

3H Feedback strategy
    approaching potential beta readers 81
    definition of 3H Beta Reading 8
    listening to your instincts 119
    reacting to beta reports 116
    relevance to breathing space 68

A

academic feedback 15
agent. *See* literary agent
alpha reader 15
analytical 121
anxious 130

B

beta readers
    chosen randomly 27
    family members 30, 44–45
    finding specialists 45–51
    large beta testing teams 51
    non-writers 13
big issues 36, 99
big-picture feedback 62, 65
breathing space, importance of 63, 68

C

character 42, 43, 60, 68, 123
children's books 13, 16, 28, 47
chocolate, importance of 29, 68, 114
clarity 14, 112, 125
coach, writing 62
competitions & contests 51, 79
conflicting reactions from beta readers
    importance of taking time to reflect 117
    looking for hidden common features in conflicting reactions 120
    normal to receive contradictory responses 116
    retaining control of the manuscript 24
    weighing the value of conflicting responses 121
    working through controversial issues 121
copy editing 20, 21, 22, 66, 71, 99
cover design 73
creative non-fiction 16, 21
criticism
    how to respond to criticism 114
    resolving confusion 124
criticism, how to deliver 62, 64, 67, 94, 114, 115

D

demographics, choosing beta readers by 26, 27
description 78, 84

detailed feedback 4, 37, 61, 62, 65, 66, 71, 97, 99, 129, 130, 131
   whether to ask for it 66
developmental feedback and editing 10, 12, 18
dialogue 63, 123, 129
different opinions. *See* conflicting reactions
disagreeing with your beta reader 117
distance, importance of getting distance from your manuscript 63, 64, 75, 115, 118

E

editor 5, 6, 10, 12, 13, 14, 17, 21, 25, 26, 43, 56, 58, 60, 62, 64, 66, 70, 72, 110
encouragement 5, 6, 86

F

Facebook, meeting beta readers 42
family members, asking them for feedback 30, 44–45
feedback phases flowchart 56
fiction 35, 45, 58, 60, 67, 83, 98, 109, 128, 129
   definition 16
first draft 63, 64, 69, 75
flattery 9
flowchart, seven feedback phases. *See* feedback phases flowchart

G

grammar 37, 63, 71, 129

H

hate, if they hate your manuscript 87, 118
heart 8, 9, 68, 82, 116, 117, 119
honesty 8, 80, 116
humility 8, 80, 117, 119

I

indie publishing 6, 21, 71, 72
instinct, value of 32, 119
intuitive 121, 123

L

large beta testing team, ways to use 51
life story. *See* memoir
LinkedIn, meeting beta readers 43
literary agent 9, 35, 71

M

marketing 104, 108
meaning 70, 123
memoir 97, 125, 127
   dealing with feedback about your personal life 63
   definition 16
   getting very early feedback on memoir 59
   how I chose a beta reader team for memoir 35
   the value of having extra beta readers for mem-

oir 67
mistake 5, 10, 68

N

non-fiction 13, 16, 17, 21, 28, 30, 33, 35, 44, 59, 60, 67, 129
   definition 16
novel. *See* fiction

P

paying for an editor 22
   versus free feedback 13, 17, 58
plot 33, 48, 49, 68, 69, 83, 86, 125, 128
proofreader 13, 21, 74
psychological pressure 115, 118, 131
punctuation 74

R

rewriting 61, 62, 64, 66, 68, 70, 71, 86, 91, 118, 126, 127, 128, 131
rewriting, how to make the most of it 64

S

schedule 18, 36, 78, 79, 84, 85, 94, 125, 130
self-editing 128
self-publishing 35, 71, 73
setting 85, 88, 94, 123
slow. *See* schedule
specialty issues 45–51, 50
strengths 5, 29, 37, 43, 86, 103, 104, 112, 120
structure 5, 33, 66, 79, 86, 96, 129
survey 4, 7, 27, 28, 29, 85, 89, 93

T

target reader 13, 28, 121
   how to define 28
thanking beta readers 129
theme 33, 105, 109, 123, 127, 128, 129
time. *See* schedule
timeframe. *See* schedule
topic 60
Track Changes, Microsoft Word 72, 90, 99
trauma
   trigger warnings 81
true story. *See* memoir; *See* non-fiction
trust 119
Twitter, meeting beta readers 42
typos, when to fix 4, 34, 62, 63, 65, 129

V

voice, author's 9, 14, 25, 33, 71, 128

W

weaknesses 104, 112
word count 78
Word (Microsoft Word) 72, 73, 78, 84, 87, 88, 89, 90, 94, 109, 110, 122
writers' groups 15, 41

About the Author

Belinda Pollard is an award-winning Australian author, publishing consultant, book editor, speaker, blogger and former journalist. She has degrees in Communication and Theology, and twenty years' experience in the publishing world, working with both traditional publishers and self-publishers.  She is an accredited member of the Institute of Professional Editors (IPEd).

Her editing portfolio includes books that have won or been shortlisted for significant awards and been translated into other languages. Some have become classics in their niche and remained continuously in print for decades.

She has more than 10,000 Twitter followers, many thousands of visitors per month to her blog at smallbluedog.com, and receives Australian and international publishing and speaking invitations as a result of her advocacy for writers and editors.

As an author, Belinda writes the Wild Crimes murder mysteries, humorous memoir, biblical meditations, and resources for writers. Her writing prizes include a Varuna Fellowship.

Connect with Belinda on Twitter, Facebook, Instagram and LinkedIn.

Visit Belinda's blogs:

- Writing and publishing tips: smallbluedog.com
- Author blog: belindapollard.com
- Christians who write for mainstream readers: gracewriters.com

Fun and useful gifts for beta readers and writers

Honor your beta readers or delight your writer friends. Choose from:

- mugs
- book bags
- pencil cases
- notebooks
- t-shirts
- even a clock!

Check out the many options at: **smallbluedog.com/gifts**

Also by Belinda Pollard

Dogged Optimism

Lessons in Joy from a Disaster-Prone Dog

ISBN: 978-0-9942098-3-2

Available in paperback, large print paperback, and ebook

For anyone who ever loved a pet or needed a laugh…

In this humorous and uplifting read, Belinda recounts how her scruffy Aussie terrier, Killarney, has helped her through the toughest of days—and taught her to make the most of life.

Killarney is not afraid of anything that sub-tropical Australia can throw at her: venomous creatures, cancer, very large dogs. She becomes Belinda's furry comforter and cheer squad through job loss, grief, and failed romance.

You will be inspired by Killarney's motto: grab life by the throat and shake every last drop of joy out of it. Wrestle it, if you have to.

"*Dogged Optimism* is an accomplished, inspiring piece of writing that had me completely hooked from the first page to the unexpected and gratifying end." Gill Pavey, thebookreviewers.com

"A delightful read, as much about the ups and downs of owning a willful dog as facing up to life, especially when it doesn't turn out as expected." Marianne Wheelaghan, *The Blue Suitcase*

"Anyone who's ever adored a dog can relate to this evocative, humorous tale." Molly Greene, The Gen Delacourt Mysteries

"Will charm you with its window into life Down Under and inspire you with its insights into overcoming personal challenges." Dawn Dicker, Writer & Content Strategist

"A heart-warming tale of one woman's special bond with her four-legged friend." Tanya Arnold, Pupcake Queen

Poison Bay

Wild Crimes #1

Varuna Fellowship winner

ISBN: 978-0-9942098-0-1

Available in paperback, large print paperback, and ebook

When the wilderness is not your only enemy, who do you trust?

Television reporter Callie Brown likes big cities and good coffee. But, running from a broken heart, she agrees to join old friends at the strangest of reunions: a trek into New Zealand's most savage and remote mountains. What she doesn't know is that someone wants them all dead...

"Taut suspense and lush descriptions." Literary Inklings

"Satisfyingly insightful." Margaret Newman

"By turns shocking, satisfying, tragic, and poignant, but ultimately life-affirming." Debbie Young's Reading Life

"So far this is my favorite fiction read of the year." Clare O'Beara, Amazon UK Top 500 Reviewer

Also available in German in paperback and ebook as

Verschollen in der Poison Bay

ISBN: 978-0-9942098-7-0

COMING SOON

Venom Reef

Wild Crimes #2

The ocean gives... and the ocean takes.

When medical researchers collide with eco-terrorists on Australia's Great Barrier Reef, who will survive?

www.ingramcontent.com/pod-product-compliance
Lightning Source LLC
Chambersburg PA
CBHW072042290426
44110CB00014B/1555